To Seth
from
Ruth

Christmas 1942.

PERSONALITIES OF THE PASSION

PERSONALITIES
OF THE PASSION

A Devotional Study of Some of the
Characters Who Played a Part in the
Drama of Christ's Passion
and Resurrection

By

LESLIE D. WEATHERHEAD

"Were you there when they crucified my Lord?"

ABINGDON-COKESBURY PRESS
New York ● *Nashville*

PERSONALITIES OF THE PASSION
COPYRIGHT, MCMXLIII
By WHITMORE & STONE

43-51047

SET UP, PRINTED, AND BOUND BY THE PARTHENON PRESS AT NASHVILLE, TENNESSEE, UNITED STATES OF AMERICA

DEDICATED
TO
MY UNCLE
THE VERY REV. JAMES WEATHERHEAD
M.A., D.D.
(St. Paul's, Dundee)
Ex-Moderator, United Free Church of Scotland
IN GRATITUDE AND AFFECTION

PREFACE

It is wonderful to the Christian preacher to find how relevant is the Gospel message to the days through which we are passing—and, further, that the darker the days the more relevant is the Gospel.

One need not "preach about the war." People ask sometimes if one does or is going to do so. They usually hope for the answer "No!" I find myself rarely doing that in the sense generally understood. But no great truth about God is irrelevant to men in great need, least of all the greatest truth of all, which shines through the drama of the passion and resurrection of the Saviour.

The Gospel was first proclaimed in a world full of turmoil and unrest and the clash of arms. Rome spelled dictatorship. Rebellion was put down at once with pitiless might and crushing force. The background of the Gospel is not completely painted in the words we often sing:

> O Sabbath rest by Galilee!
> O calm of hills above,
> Where Jesus knelt to share with Thee
> The silence of eternity
> Interpreted by love!

I like that hymn more than most. But, though unwillingly sometimes, I remind myself that dotted

7

round the shores of Galilee were no less than ten industrial towns of at least fifteen thousand inhabitants each—towns packed with explosive feelings ready to be touched off into blazing revolt by a spark from the endless discussions or a sword suddenly unsheathed—and that the "hills above" were the lairs and hiding places of bandits and brigands who made journeys hazardous and possession a risk.

The background of the drama of the Passion must be looked at anew. Then, watching the stage of Jewish history at its most tragic period, we shall hear sudden, wild alarms, the clash of arms by night, furtive plottings and counterplottings, strange movements of influential men at midnight; we shall see the glint of moonlight on swords in a shadowed garden, hear a fisherman swearing in a strange guttural accent by a fire in a courtyard, watch a man fleeing from his own conscience, and a sad procession moving slowly along the way of sorrow—a procession not yet ended. And then that Awful Climax, which still makes men wonder and think and pray and repent all over the world, and finally the ecstatic aftermath of incredible joy—dawn in another garden among flowers and bird song, a dawn of peace, a sunrise never again quite overcast with clouds, not even now, in this dark storm of the world.

It seems more fitting now than ever it was to read again the drama of the Cross, with universal sorrow all around us, in a world where ideologies are clash-

ing and crashing, where men are drilling and daring
and groaning and dying, and women are weeping
and worrying and moaning and mourning; where all
are looking and hoping and watching for a day of
resurrection after the death of so much that was
dear.

I suppose you *could* read about the Crucifixion
lying, cigarette or chocolate in mouth, on the cushions
of a punt, moored under the trees in some quiet
backwater, or among the reeds at the edge of a lake,
on some drowsy Sunday afternoon in August with
no sound but the lapping water and the drone of
bees. Swinburne's poems fit into that:

> From too much love of living,
>   From hope and fear set free,
> We thank with brief thanksgiving
>   Whatever gods may be,
> That no life lives for ever;
> That dead men rise up never;
> That even the weariest river
>   Winds somewhere safe to sea.

But not the Cross.   The Cross does not fit that mood.
I am writing for men and women with boys away
at war; for some with boys who will never come
back from war; for people with girls serving at home
or abroad; for people with children evacuated and
homes silent; for men with businesses they've worked

all their lives to build up dropping to pieces, though they're working as they never worked before; for women with household cares and problems that nearly drive them crazy. I'm writing for some with bombed homes and bombed businesses and bombed churches and bombed hearts, and perhaps a bombed faith.

They are in the mood, I think, to look at the sad glory of the Cross.

This little book, of course, makes no attempt to study all that is implied for life and thought in the dying of Jesus. But I have been helped to enter the right mood for both worship and understanding by trying to look at the central act of the whole drama of human history from the point of view of those who played some part in it. Those would get most out of the book, I think, who would read thoughtfully the scripture passages referred to in the footnotes—I have overburdened the book with footnotes!—and who would not reject this interpretation or that as fanciful until at least they had tried to read the Gospel story as though they had never heard it before, and certainly never heard it before read as "lessons" in church in a voice that killed its liveness and vivid poignancy.

The substance of these chapters has been given in Lenten addresses in the City Temple, London. At the end of each address there was an interval of silent prayer, during which the City Temple organist, my good friend, Mr. Martin Fearn, briefly extemporized very quietly on the theme "Were you there when they crucified my Lord?" For me, and I think for all, this greatly added to the beauty of the service, and it certainly thrust the message home. The address on "Joseph of Arimathea" was given at the Easter morning service, 1941, on the Sunday before the church was destroyed by bombs. As two thousand people sang for the last time in that great building,

> Christ the Lord is risen today,
> Alleluia!

no one suspected how badly we should need the comfort of the Easter message before the week was out. Early the following Thursday morning the building was gutted by fire from incendiary bombs dropped from enemy planes, but the next Sunday morning a friend of mine, approaching the hall lent to us for temporary worship, heard my beloved and faithful people singing:

> Lead us, heavenly Father, lead us
>   O'er the world's tempestuous sea;
> Guard us, guide us, keep us, feed us,
>   For we have no help but Thee,
> Yet possessing every blessing,
>   If our God our Father be.

The chapter on "Peter" appeared in a shortened form in the *Christian World*. The one on "Caiaphas" was included in part xxiii of the series *In His Steps*, "The Crucifixion in Sacred Art," published by the Amalgamated Press, Limited. The substance of the last chapter appeared in a volume published by James Clarke and Company, entitled *Festival Sermons*. I am grateful for permission to use some of this material again, though each chapter has been entirely rewritten.

My obligation to books is acknowledged in footnotes so far as this has been practicable.

I am deeply indebted to three friends who have read the proofs and helped me both by suggestions and in the laborious detail of preparing a book for the press: Mr. Albert Clare, my church secretary, treasurer, editor of the *City Temple Tidings,* and author of our official history, *The City Temple, 1640-1940;* Mr. Ronald Ward, of New College, London University; and Miss Winifred E. Haddon, my devoted and able secretary.

LESLIE D. WEATHERHEAD

CONTENTS

13

Chapter I

PETER

ONE evening I was doing what I have always found to be of great value, trying to read a portion of the New Testament as though I had never read it before. The portion was the fourteenth chapter of Mark, and I read the words: "Jesus saith unto him [Peter], Verily I say unto thee, that thou today, even this night, before the cock crow twice, shalt deny me thrice." My mind was arrested by a sense of certainty that Jesus could not possibly have meant those words to be taken in the way I had always supposed. For if there is one way of undermining the loyalty of a friend which is more certain than another, it is to let him know, quite definitely, that you don't believe he will maintain his loyalty, and, indeed, that he is bound to fail. Take away the familiar language of the Gospel and we have something like this: "*You* are no good. Before the night is through, *you* will have let me down." Jesus would never have given to a chosen and loyal, if impulsive, follower such a bad suggestion as that. Nor can we in these days imagine that Peter was predestined to deny Jesus three times in the sense of filling an inescapable role, or that Jesus was foretelling something that was bound, inevitably, to happen, irrespective of Peter's will.

We therefore need to look at this incident a little more closely. Matthew, Luke, and John all say, "Before the cock crow [at all], thou shalt deny me thrice";[1] but we know that Mark's Gospel reveals most closely the mind of Peter, since Mark probably owed the substance of his Gospel to Peter. Mark says, "Before the cock crow twice, [thou] shalt deny me thrice." Some scholars have made the attractive suggestion that the words "twice" and "thrice" may have occurred in the earliest manuscripts together, so that the sentence would read: "Before the cock crow, twice thrice shalt thou deny me." [2] This, of course, does not mean before the earliest bird opened its noisy beak, or even before one bird was answered by another—which *might* account for the word "twice." [3] It means "before the dawn." It may mean, indeed, before the bugle blows.[4] The Roman bugle, sounded from the Tower of Antony during the night at six, nine, midnight, and three A.M., was called the *gallus* or cock; and the two trumpet calls at midnight and three A.M. were both called "cock crowings" (*gallicinia*). These two calls *may* explain the word "twice." The purpose of the bugle

---

[1] Matt. 26:34; Luke 22:34; John 13:38.

[2] There is no punctuation in the early manuscripts, and it seems reasonable to insert a comma after "crow."

[3] A. E. J. Rawlinson, *The Gospel According to St. Mark,* p. 209.

[4] Some writers tell us that no cocks were allowed in Jerusalem during a feast.

was to signal for the relief of the guard, but it told the whole city the time also. We know that the word "thrice" is a Greek idiom meaning repeatedly. When Paul says, "I besought the Lord *thrice*," in relation to deliverance from his thorn in the flesh,[5] he does not mean on three occasions, but repeatedly. The expression "twice thrice"—taking the words together, unseparated by a comma—means, therefore, again and again, the whole sentence being liable to the interpretation, "Before the dawn you will have denied me again and again." [6]

Some hold tenaciously to the thought that Jesus was foretelling what Peter would do, but beyond the difficulties of the problem of Peter's free will is the important point that, if the four narratives are carefully read, it will be found that Peter denied Jesus more than three times and certainly not less than six; and I hold that the theory of prophecy in the sense generally understood makes nonsense of the mind of Jesus.[7] Besides, if he *did* know for certain that Peter would repeatedly deny him, would he

[5] II Cor. 12:8.

[6] Cf. Job 33:29 (Moffatt), "God does all this over and again, twice, thrice, for men." The Hebrew word translated "oftentimes" is literally twice, thrice.

[7] The fulfillment of a supposed prophecy was made by "adding (1) in Mark's version (14:68), the clause 'and the cock crew,' which the best authorities omit (cf. R. V. margin), and (2) 'the second time' or 'straightway the second time' in verse 72 where the earliest manuscripts have 'straightway'"; cf. David Smith, *Commentary on the Four Gospels*, II, 128.

have chosen that moment grimly to have told Peter so in front of the others?

But we are not much further; for the sentence as we have translated it, "Before the dawn you will deny me repeatedly," is still a bad psychological suggestion, likely to undermine Peter's loyalty. Certain as I am that Jesus would not do that, I fall back on the fact that no New Testament writer has recorded the expression on Jesus' face. Kahlil Gibran, in his book *Jesus, the Son of Man,* says, "Jesus put his hand upon Peter's shoulder and smiled upon him, and said, 'Who knows but that you may deny me before this night is over and leave me before I leave you?'" [8] One imagines that this interpretation conveys Jesus' meaning. Peter has impulsively said, "Although all shall be offended, yet will not I." [9] Can we not imagine Jesus, with his hand on Peter's shoulder, and a smile upon his face, saying very tenderly, "My dear fellow, I should not be surprised if, before the dawn, you had done it half a dozen times"?

What is Peter's reaction? I think the natural reaction of this lovable, impulsive man would be, in the same spirit of camaraderie, to say to himself, "He knows I am impulsive and a bit of a wobbler. I will prove to him that I can be as brave as any." And whatever we like to say about Peter's denial,

[8] P. 197.
[9] Mark 14:29.

it required no ordinary courage, when the others ran away, for Peter to follow "to see the end";[10] and I, for one, do not believe that Peter did deny Jesus. I believe that when he followed to the courtyard it was not a kind of attenuated loyalty or lingering love making him unwilling to be arrested with him and yet unwilling to desert him. I think Peter was seeking information. As many another has done in a great cause, before and since, he was playing the part of a spy. Either he had the intention of rescuing Jesus or else of hearing what was likely to become of him so that a possible rescue could be considered. If it were merely a kind of attenuated loyalty, would he not have kept in the dark shadows of the courtyard? Instead of that he comes right up to the fire. "When they had kindled a fire in the midst of the court, and had sat down together, Peter sat in the midst of them."[11] I think he was by the fire to listen to what the others said and gather what news he could. Then someone throws a handful of thorns—like those from which the crown of thorns was woven—on the fire. The flames leap up. A maid's bright eyes espy him. For a moment she does not speak. She has the feeling, common to us all, of having seen a person somewhere and not being quite sure where. Then with a flash of her eyes she says, "You were with him, too."

[10] See Matt. 26:58.
[11] Luke 22:55.

Before we consider Peter's answer, let us imagine a British spy disguised as a German, taken prisoner during the war, in German territory. If he were challenged, would anyone on this earth expect him to say, "Yes, I am really an Englishman masquerading as a German"? If he said, "I am a German like yourself, and I hate the English," would anyone in his senses accuse him of *denying* his country? His "denial" at that point is the highest service he can render to his country.

Here is Peter acting the part of a spy. What sort of a spy is it who, as soon as he is challenged, throws up his hands and says, "Yes, of course, I was with him"? When he says definitely, "I neither know, nor understand what thou sayest," [12] Peter is merely playing his part. I refuse to call that a denial. Unfortunately, poor old Peter forgets to disguise his voice. He has the fatal Galilean accent which, Mr. Gossip tells us in his book of that title,[13] was unmistakable in the way that the gutturals were slurred and the syllables swallowed. So Peter was in the position of a Scot surrounded by Londoners and saying, "Ye dinna ken what ye're ta'king aboot." His accent gives him away at once, and then he loses his head and does what a man often does who loses his head; he begins to curse and swear and to keep on repeating, obstinately, his former statement.

[12] Mark 14:68.
[13] *The Galilean Accent*, p. 1.

The maid, or maids, evidently saw him again—
Matthew says "another maid." Evidently the girls
would not leave him alone, nor the men either. The
Fourth Gospel says that a kinsman of the man whose
ear Peter cut off teased him also,[14] and Peter got
terribly confused. They baited him till he was terrified. Already he was wounded to the quick to think
that his accent had made him fail. Intending only
to help, he seemed to have made a terrible mess of
it; and, as the first streak of dawn lit up the sky and
the trumpets sounded, Peter remembered the words
of Jesus, and his humiliation was complete.

Then we may imagine Jesus, in charge of his
guards, passing near and looking at Peter. Probably
Jesus had overheard the baiting of Peter, and he
turned and looked upon him. But whence comes the
idea that Jesus' look was a look of rebuke? The
fact that "the Lord turned, and looked upon Peter"
is recorded only by Luke.[15] There is not the slightest
hint in the Gospels that it was a look of rebuke. Indeed, I feel quite sure in my mind that it was a look
of tenderness; for if one is emotionally very worked
up and tense, a look of rebuke does not induce tears.
It might induce profound regret. It would be more
likely to induce stonyheartedness or the bitter gall
of cynical despair. Let me ask the reader a question: When you are keyed up almost to the breaking

[14] John 18:26.
[15] Luke 22:61.

point, is it the cold look of rebuke that moves you? I think not. But if somebody is kind, you break down at once. Indeed, many people at a time of great mental stress have said to me, "Now, don't speak kindly to me or else I shall cry." Surely Jesus understood the loving loyalty of his friend. Jesus probably did not *desire* Peter to act as a spy and to maintain the role so stubbornly with what some people would call lies. Jesus probably was not asking that his beloved Peter should eavesdrop in preparation for a rescue. But Jesus would know how to accept even the misplaced affection of his own man, and Jesus turned on him with a look full of loving understanding and sympathy that said more eloquently than words, "Never mind, Peter, I know exactly how you feel and what you intended to do." It was the smile of reassurance and kindly sympathy, and it broke Peter down into tears, because, meaning to be loyal and brave and do his Master a service, he had made such a mess of things.

The risen Lord continued this ministry of reassurance to Peter, the man who tried and meant so earnestly to succeed. The message came from the lips of Mark—if, as seems likely, Mark was the young man inside the tomb—"Go, tell his disciples *and Peter.*" If Peter had really denied Jesus, would he have gone back to the ten? Judas went and hanged himself. But however Peter had blundered, his conscience did not hold him guilty of anything but losing his head in a misguided attempt to serve his Master.[16]

But another point must be considered. Peter, on the Day of Pentecost, preached to people who knew all, and some of whom were present at the Crucifixion[17]—people who knew the facts at first hand. And he says to them of Jesus, "Ye by the hand of lawless men did crucify and slay." Is it possible that he could say that to others if he himself had denied his Lord? Anyone in the crowd might have shouted, "What about you? You denied him yourself."

It is interesting, in passing, to notice how the very taunts of the New Testament have sometimes become tributes. They said of Jesus that "he was the friend of publicans and sinners." Dr. T. R. Glover has called that "the most precious slander that ever oozed from slimy lips." They also said of him that "he saved others; himself he cannot save." What greater tribute could ever be paid to the whole nature of love than that? And here is a maid who says to Peter, "You were there. You have been with him; your accent betrays you."

There are some of us who, if that could be said of us, would feel it to be the greatest honor that could possibly come our way. For there is an accent of the soul which gives away, to all who hear it, where

[16] Does the fullness with which the story is told in the Second Gospel suggest that Peter tried to make this clear to Mark?

[17] Acts 2:22.

the soul has lived. If someone overheard you speaking to your children, or to the maid, or to a man at the door, or to a customer, or to an employee, or to a class of boys, or to the man next to you in the bus, or in a pulpit, or in an office, or mine, or factory, or workshop, or a deacons' meeting, and if in his heart that someone said, "He has been with Jesus. His speech betrays him," would not this be the greatest compliment in the world?

This accent of the soul is not only heard in our speech, but betrayed in our eyes, in our laughter, in our whole attitude to life. Many of us are laboriously trying to use the Galilean language, and it is well worth all our efforts to do so. But let me imagine for a moment that your boy is learning French. He is laboriously translating sentences like this: "Have you pens, ink, and paper?" "Yes, but I have no apples." "Has the son of the gardener any marbles?" "No, but he has three books." So we may, in some sense, learn French! But if you had enough money you would probably send your boy, later on, to France. Let him hear nothing else but the French language and he will speak it much more quickly and with the correct accent. Do we want those whose lives touch ours to learn the Galilean language? Then I suggest that the best way of teaching them is never to let them hear anything else. And if we ourselves want to be like Jesus, remind others of him, and speak the language of the soul which he

spoke, speak it with our eyes, and handclasp and ac-
tions, as well as with our voices, it is not enough to
have Christian teachers.   So many of them speak it
badly, halting and stuttering in their speech.   He
alone speaks it perfectly, and we must go to him.

But there is a further point.   Can we ever hope to
show forth the spirit of Christ, to speak fluently and
from the heart?   The answer depends on whether
this is a new language we have to learn, or the true
native language of the soul.   Wordsworth and Plato
would suggest the latter: that we were born dreaming
in this language, that when we look on beauty it reminds us of our true home, that we are not setting
out to learn a strange tongue.   Deep in the mind are
"those shadowy recollections" of which Wordsworth
wrote.   We are in a far country, some of us, or
traveling very slowly out of it, and we have forgotten the language of the homeland; but as we come
back we shall find a strange familiarity, like a High-
lander, long exiled in London, returning at last to
his village amid the Scottish hills.   The more we
dwell with Christ, the sooner shall we come into that
Kingdom of the Spirit which is our true home, where
what we might call the Galilean language is most
spoken.   And at last we shall wear as a garland the
taunt of a maid which is now the highest praise in
the world, "Thou also wert with him.   Thy speech
betrayeth thee."

Chapter II

JUDAS

W E turn now to the study of the personality of Judas Iscariot, one of the most tragic personalities in history, and, to my mind, one of the most misunderstood. From the very beginning Judas was a lonely man. In any estimate of his character we must try to realize that. He came from Kerioth, which was down in the south of Judea, and he was the only one of the twelve who was not a Galilean.

In trying to come to some understanding of his personality I think there are some things which we can dismiss.

First, we can dismiss the idea that Judas was a puppet, predestined to play a certain part in the betrayal of Christ; and that Christ, sharing the foreknowledge of God, chose him, knowing from the very beginning that by Judas he would be betrayed. There are some people still who believe in what they call the "plan of salvation." They believe that the death of Christ was determined and that every act in that terrible drama was decreed beforehand in a way that made the sin of Judas a divine necessity. That it is God's will to *allow* evil is clear. Without the possibility of man's choice of evil, his good would be without moral value. To say that the action of

26

Judas was "within the will of God" is justifiable if we mean that God both foreknew it and allowed it. But it is, I think, useful to distinguish between what God allows and what God intends. To suggest that it was God's intention that a man in a divine drama should do evil, and, indeed, that he had no real freedom to do otherwise, makes God a partaker in evil, which is impossible, and makes Judas free from blame. Judas, like all men, within certain limits was a free agent, else the will of God and the will of Judas would be the same thing, which again is impossible. The fact that the whole drama of the Crucifixion was known to God from all eternity does not spell determinism. It means that he knew what men would do with their free will. Our doing conditions his knowing. His knowing does not condition our doing. I will not try to deal here with the difficulty at great length. I believe that Judas was a free agent who fell deeply into sin, though not in the way generally understood. And I believe that the murder of Christ was not the intention of God any more than any other murder in history or any other evil can be said to be the intention of God. We will not now be drawn into a discussion of the Atonement. Suffice it to say that the Cross means what it does mean not because an evil deed was essential to that great doing, but that there was a divine deed done in spite of and through the evil purposes of men. Calvary speaks to us, not through those who plotted and schemed to bring it about, but through him who hung upon it, through what he accomplished there, and because he who won that victory was the unique Son of God. So let us banish from our minds the thought of Judas as a mere necessary pawn in a game.

In the second place let us exclude the emphasis that has been placed upon the greed of Judas. I cannot avoid the feeling that after the terrible events of the Cross, the evangelists could not make Judas black enough. So John, writing late, says (12:6), "He was a thief, and having the bag took away what was put therein." And, of course, there must have been some evidence for such a statement. Yet I have a strange stop in my mind at believing this about Judas, because Jesus was a very clear reader of personality, and would he make his treasurer the man who, more than anybody else, was tempted to rob? Further, if a man is very weak on that side of his nature, if he is covetous and greedy, as John makes out, is he the kind of man to attach himself to a band of wandering preachers who, if the phrase may be allowed, have hardly a bean between them? He could not possibly have made more than a few shillings, and where would he spend it? What would he do with it? When a man is down there are always plenty of people who will stamp on him as they pass, and though I am open to be shown that I am wrong, I cannot avoid the conclusion that that is what has happened in the case of Judas. The evangelists keep adding, whenever they mention his name, "who also betrayed him." [1] John alludes to him as "the son of perdition." Are they making him the scapegoat of their own shortcomings? If one man in a group is painted very black, the grayness of the rest is white by comparison. Samuel Butler reminds us that it is an old trick of the mind for men to

> Compound for sins they are inclin'd to,
> By damning those they have no mind to.[2]

Perhaps, also, we ought to take account of the false idea that handling money was supposed to be a lower form of service than the work which the other disciples were doing. In modern days one often hears people say in a meeting, "Now let us turn to the more spiritual part of our work." Yet surely the careful handling of finance is a necessary and, if we have our sense of values right, a spiritual part of Christian work. Jesus, it is believed, was maintained by the contributions of a committee in Jerusalem which disbursed sums of money, mainly contributed by wealthy widows, for the use of any traveling rabbi whose credentials were in order. That necessitated the keeping of a purse, and that necessitated the appointment of a treasurer. Here is the man Judas, who, after all, like the rest, has left

[1] Matt. 10:4; Mark 3:19; Luke 6:16; John 18:2.
[2] "Hudibras."

his home and friends and business for a great ideal, and who, for obvious reasons, could not have done that for what he was going to get out of it. And I imagine that he may have pilfered certain small sums or been unable to balance his accounts and that this was recalled against him by those who were only too ready to dub him as utterly wicked.

This point leads us to the third thing that I should like to exclude, and that is the supposition that Judas was a terribly wicked man. I have been reading some old commentaries and am amazed at the phrases which are used concerning Judas. "Satanic wickedness." [3] "Horrible and diabolical." [4] These are the kind of things that are said, and I don't want to exonerate Judas or whitewash him. That would be to make as great a mistake in the opposite direction. But I do want us to understand him and to realize that we have done much the same kind of thing ourselves. In a sentence, the sins that brought Jesus to the Cross were not diabolical crimes. They were the sins of the kind of people like you and me.

For my own part I refuse to believe that any man could live closely in touch with Jesus for over two years, and then go out in cold blood and sell him to his enemies for the mere motive of money. The sum that Judas received is an answer to the charge of cupidity. Thirty pieces of silver were worth a little

[3] Bruce, *The Training of the Twelve*, p. 358.
[4] Hastings, *Dictionary of the Bible*, p. 502.

over four pounds in our money. It was the amount
recoverable by a slave who had been beaten by his
master until the blood ran. If Judas had been the
grasping, greedy man we sometimes suppose, he
could have made five or six times that amount from
the priests.

May I then, having criticized some current conceptions, try to paint Judas as I see him? Following
other writers, I see this lonely, Judean young man as
the passionate nationalist of the little band. His
patriotism is the fanatical kind which we used to
associate, for instance, with the Sinn Fein movement
in Ireland. The words "Sinn Fein" mean, I am told,
"Ourselves Alone." And Judas was possessed by
the narrow, intolerant nationalist spirit which, I am
afraid, is one of the most dread diseases of our
civilization and one of the greatest menaces of the
international situation; a form of intolerant selfishness that is a perversion of patriotism rather than the
real thing. I believe that Jesus himself was a patriot.
In fact, to be a Jew was to be a patriot. But Jesus
had seen a far greater vision than Judas saw. Jesus
had seen a vision in the desert, not of a Rome
banished and driven into the sea and a worldly kingdom for the Jews. He had seen all the kingdoms of
this world and their glory as his Father's kingdom,
in a sublimation of patriotism in which there was
neither Greek nor Jew, nor Barbarian nor Roman,
nor any division whatever, but all one in the willing

service of God the Father of all. Now Judas had never seen that vision. On the other hand, what he *did* see was his beloved Master with power at his finger tips such as no man had ever possessed. I believe that Judas thought of Jesus definitely as the Messiah. Moreover, just the kind of Messiah in which he, Judas, had reveled. A Messiah who could do many mighty works and wonderful deeds: the very idol of the Old Testament poets and seers, and the perfect realization of all the prophetic dreams. I believe it was this conception of Jesus which had swept Judas the patriot, Judas the passionate in blood, and impulsive in temper, into the ranks of Christ's followers. After all, was not one of Christ's own temptations that of acting in the way Judas wished him to do? [5]

Then a slow process of disappointment and disillusionment set in, and the whole psychology of Judas became, to my mind, the psychology of a man in whom impatience has gone mad. One can almost hear him say to himself, "Why doesn't he get a move on? If I had a tenth of the power that he has, I would not waste my time healing beggars and talking to blind men by the roadside; wasting an hour with a woman at midday and with a man at midnight! This lingering and wasting of time with ones and twos is ridiculous. Why doesn't he start a great movement? Why doesn't he use his power?

[5] Luke 4:5-6.

Why doesn't he sweep Rome into the sea and set up the kingdom of his ancestor David? He has shown that he is not only supreme over things natural but things supernatural. If he raised his little finger all the young men in Palestine with red blood in their veins would rise to his call. Nothing could withstand him. He can even raise people from the dead. And here he is fleeing from one place to another, talking about this mad idea of love, babbling about a cross, saying that he must suffer. Why doesn't he *act?*"

So, disappointed, thwarted, fanatical, mad, Judas wonders how he can force the hand of Jesus. "His hope was," says De Quincey, "that Christ would no longer vacillate; he would be forced into giving the signal to the populace of Jerusalem who would then rise unanimously." Doubts have become more common in Judas' mind and his ultimate argument is this. "If he *is* the Messiah, nothing can hurt him, and if I force his hand and make him act he will sweep all before him. If he is not the Messiah the sooner it is all over the better." But Judas believed he *was*. Thus this man, rapidly becoming what we should today call a "psychotic," argued. There is an old tradition that Judas was a man of distinguished birth and had friends in high places. I wonder if they had taunted him. I wonder whether he went to them in this spirit: "Very well, put him to the test; you try to take him. I will show you where he

prays. I will lead you straight to him, and the man
I kiss is your man." I wonder if he said under his
breath, "And then you will see whether he is a king
or not." And perhaps, then, they said, "Well, that is
a good idea. Here is five pounds for your trouble,"
and Judas, weak on that side, took the money. If
Judas had not painted Jesus to the priests as a man
of tremendous and supernatural *power,* surely they
would not have paid him a penny. They paid because they were afraid of Jesus. Judas made them
afraid. But for that fear, surely they would not
have to pay money before they could effect the arrest
of a wandering preacher. They were afraid of his
supernatural power *and a revolution among the people*. They paid Judas to tell them when arrest would
be easy and secret.

I don't believe, for a single moment, that Judas
ever dreamed that Jesus would allow himself to be
put to death. If you had seen a Person raise people
from the dead, would you imagine that that Person
would allow himself to be murdered? And, of
course, the idea of a triumph, in spite of and by
means of the Cross, was as far from Judas' mind as,
quite frankly, it is from the mind of the modern
man.

So Judas, his eyes wild, his mind racing, goes to
the Upper Room for the Last Supper just in the
faint hope that even yet Jesus may be going to an-
nounce a policy which fitted in with Judas' idea of

how a Messiah should act. But Jesus only talks
about a body broken and of blood shed. He hears
the fateful words, "One of you shall betray me."
Does he not feel, even then, "Ah! you won't call it
betrayal because it will all work out all right and you
will see that I was right after all"? So he seeks out
the authorities and himself guides the temple police
to the place in the garden where his Master prays.
Can you see Judas, his hair disheveled, his wild eyes
blazing and bulging out of their sockets, his whole
being in utter tumult? And can you see the calm
face of Jesus with those burning, quiet, awful eyes,
and the voice that said, "Friend, do what you came
to do"? This is not the story of satanic wickedness;
it is the story of one who utterly misunderstood.
And perhaps those words of Jesus are a last appeal
to Judas. Prof. J. A. Findlay tells us that cups,
similar to those used at the Last Supper and of the
same period, have been unearthed and that on their
base was discovered an inscription bearing the words,
"Do what you came to do," which might have been
a motto of the time as common as our motto, "Do it
now." What if the Master made one last appeal to
Judas by quoting to him the motto on the cup from
which they had both drunk? Jesus sees that it is impossible now to make Judas understand, and the
Master is taken and hurried away to trial and then
to death.

We must, I think, look at Judas tenderly. He is

almost mad now, if not completely so. He never
dreamed that Jesus would let himself be taken. He
rushes back to the priests in the temple, flings their
money down—no mere thief this—and, in a horror
that we shall never understand, says, "I have sinned.
I have betrayed innocent blood." You notice the cold,
callous cynicism of the priests—priests who every
day offered sacrifice in the temple for penitent sinners
that they might be received of God! They received
this penitent, broken, frantic man, and drove the cold
steel knife of their sarcasm into his hot heart. "What
is that to us?" they said, "that is your affair." That
contempt was the strength of the rope that hanged
him, for then his mind snapped. There was a field.
Did he not know it well enough; had he not noticed
again and again the curious configuration of a
stunted, gnarled old tree, standing alone in the
middle of the field—a field which he easily purchased
—and perhaps, because it was subject to strong pre-
vailing winds, was bent over by the blasts till it took
on the similitude of a pointing, accusing finger? Or
was it a finger pointing the only way out, a signpost
directing him to the only road left for him to travel?
At the foot of the tree was a gray rock. He had
noticed a thousand times the rock and the tree in
the middle of this field. There was something awesome about that blasted trunk and that gray rock,
half as old as time. Boys often climbed up on the
rock and crawled along the trunk of the tree, and,

swinging from the hands, dropped on to the ground below. It was not a very big drop, but it would be enough. Judas has been rushing like a man in a nightmare from one friend to another trying every means now of rescuing Jesus, but without avail. At last he learns that crucifixion is inevitable. Blinding tears burst from his eyes. He is rushing through a night that seems as though it will never end. His fingers are undoing the girdle that binds his robe round his waist. A gleam of moonlight suddenly lights up this tree, with its unfaltering, inescapable, pointing finger. He has undone his girdle now, fastened it securely round his throat, made of the other end a great loop. He is up on the rock, crawling along the branch, has slipped the noose end over the hook made by a broken branch, and then he hurls himself down. The girdle breaks—a man's girdle is not very strong and Judas is a heavy man—but not before it has taken away his life; and he falls on to the stones below, suffering the terrible injuries that are described in the first chapter of Acts.[6] I wonder if that last act revealed what some would call "the psychotic motive"? Jesus had called him—"Follow me." And now Jesus was dead. And Judas, never dreaming he would let himself be taken, had brought him to the cross. All he could do was to follow the Master he still loved—into the other world.

[6] Acts 1:18, "Falling headlong, he burst asunder in the midst, and all his bowels gushed out."

And into that unseen world, in imagination, we may follow. He who spoke so tenderly to a dying revolutionary on the cross next his own would not turn away his chosen man whose brokenhearted lament must surely have been this: "I never meant to bring him to such an awful end. I never dreamed he would not use his power. It would have been so easy. The priests were already afraid of him. I only thought to force his hand and make his kingdom come." So in that other world, by the marvelous sea, two men would meet again—Jesus the Christ of God, and Judas the man who failed him because he did not understand. And I think in that other world Judas would be dazed, utterly broken, feeling himself to be a shadow of something that was unclean forever. But would there not be a hand stretched out to raise him to his feet again, and eyes that would search his very soul, "larger, other eyes than ours," seeing all the twisted motives and all the insane confusion, and yet bringing a healing peace that comes to the soul that has sinned but now is greatly forgiven? And would there not be a great light in the eyes of Jesus, made happy because all his boys now had come home, and because he had lost not one, not even the son of perdition?

Yes, I think we must think tenderly of Judas, not emphasizing the greed of the man, not supposing him dreadfully wicked; but seeing him as a hot-blooded patriot, whose nationalism Jesus wanted to sublimate into a love of the kingdom of the men of all nations; seeing him as one who let Christ down without meaning to, because he would not understand. Perhaps that is the explanation of a good many of our sins. Most of us do not deliberately plot to hurt that holy love of which Jesus is the personification and incarnation. Our instincts get out of hand though, and our selfishness grows up in the dark, and our pride seems such a precious thing to keep. We say hot, bitter, cruel, impatient words, and do unconsidered, thoughtless things. Thus we all betray him.

> O break, O break, hard heart of mine;
> Thy weak self-love and guilty pride
> His Pilate and His Judas are:
> Jesus my Lord is crucified.

But if we will turn, even now, to him, seeking the mercy which he offers and the love which can restore, then those eyes will shine upon us in utter forgiveness; that hand will be stretched out to raise us from the dust; that Divine voice will say to us the word that was said to Judas—"Friend!"

Chapter III

CAIAPHAS

WHEN we come to Caiaphas we are getting nearer to the forces of evil which drove Jesus to the cross. If the guilt can be laid upon one, then that one is not Judas or Pilate, but Caiaphas. To my own mind, Judas misunderstood, and Pilate, as we shall see later, was frightened; but in Caiaphas there is cool, calculated cunning. There is bitter, implacable hatred. No hot impulse swayed Caiaphas, no grievous misunderstanding, no mere sudden fear. Here is the cold, deadly, clever brain. Here are the glittering, steely eyes of the snake which has been watching its prey for a long time, and coiling its sinuous folds with deadly preparedness only waiting for the right moment to strike. Caiaphas is the personification of all that is despicable and foul in the insincere ecclesiastic.

Let us look at him closely. He belongs to the sect of the Sadducees, a priestly party whose earliest adherents were descendants of Zadok. The prophet Ezekiel regarded the Sadducees as the only legitimate priests. In Jesus' time scribes and Pharisees were often priests. Nor is it implied that all Sadducees were priests. But the Sadducees were aristocrats in religion, and they believed that the priests could legitimately be recruited only from their own members. It was unheard of that any but a Sadducee should become a high priest. Although the office of high priest was the appointment of Rome—much to the dislike of the Jews—yet Annas the Sadducee had so craftily pulled the wires and exerted his influence that six high priests running had been members of his own family, and Caiaphas, the seventh, was his own son-in-law.

It was openly said that Annas, a very wealthy man, had lent money to influential Romans to such an extent that he could blackmail them to do just what he wanted. Annas and Caiaphas and the other Sadducees were deep in political intrigue, for Palestine had become part of the Roman Empire, and yet the power over the people remained in the hands of the Sadducees, who were fighting for the privileges of priesthood. They cared nothing for the true religion of Jehovah. They cared only for their own prestige and power.

We generally think of the Pharisees as being the group most hostile to Jesus, but the religion of the Pharisees was a power for good in the land compared with that of the Sadducees. We sometimes need to remind ourselves of that fact. Jesus, for instance, pointing the contrast between the Pharisee and the publican praying in the temple, to the disparagement of the Pharisee and to the honor of the publican, at least paints a picture of a Pharisee who can say, "I fast twice in the week; I give tithes of all that I get." [1] And we need to be careful not to out-pharisee the Pharisee by thinking of him only with scorn. Do we discipline ourselves in any way equivalent to fasting twice in a week? I am afraid not. And if everybody gave a tenth of all he possessed to God, there would be no need for bazaars! We must remember that, though Jesus has blackened the name of the Pharisees forever, he had many friends among them, and many of them were thoroughly good men. The sect of the Pharisees, even before they were thus named, had done much for the Jewish religion, preserving its purity from the influence of surrounding cults, especially from the effects of Greek culture which Alexander sought to introduce.

Jesus had very few contacts with the Sadducees, for the simple reason that they were the aristocrats, and he usually dealt with, spoke to, and associated with the common people. Though the Sadducees were watching the developments of his movement with increasing dislike and restlessness, the wanderings of a carpenter become rabbi had not yet engaged their official attention. They were hoping that the new movement would die out without their condescending to touch it.

But the Pharisees would never have crucified Jesus. The Sadducees crucified him, and Caiaphas was their

[1] Luke 18:12.

head and their high priest;[2] and behind Caiaphas was
a more potent enemy still, Annas, his father-in-law,
who had been removed from the high priesthood, but
who still held the reins of power in his hand—an
astute, unscrupulous diplomatist, whom it would not
be unfair to describe as a wily old fiend.

The state of rottenness of the influential ecclesiasticism of Jesus' day is hard to exaggerate. We
cannot wonder at the violence of the language of
Jesus to the professional clergy with whom he came
in touch. They misrepresented the whole nature of
religion, and burdened the people with unnecessary
and finicking detail; making it, for instance, a serious
sin that a man should drag a stick along the ground
on the Sabbath because that was plowing, and plowing is breaking the Sabbath. A woman was not
allowed to use a mirror on the Sabbath. She might
espy a gray hair, and if she plucked it out she would
be guilty of reaping on the Sabbath and thus breaking it! Such a Sabbath deserved to be broken, and
we can understand Christ's passionate words to those
who in the holy name of religion made such a fuss
about details—anise, mint and cummin—and bound
on men's shoulders burdens grievous to be borne.
A thousand laws of incredible stupidity, which peo-

[2] The phrase "Caiaphas being high priest that year" (John
11:49 and 18:13) does not mean that the office was held annually by a different person, but that this was the man who was
high priest when Jesus came up for trial in the year that changed
the world's history.

ple could not possibly keep in mind, were regarded as religious observances.

But behind all that was something very much worse. Annas and Caiaphas were growing rich through the taxes they levied on the people, apart from the Roman taxes. Taxation was nearly as heavy as it is today. A third of a man's livelihood was swallowed up in meeting it. For to the Roman taxes were added the taxes imposed by the high priest. We can scarcely believe the fact, recorded by Josephus, that twenty thousand priests ministered in the temple. Some would serve in the temple for one week only in the year, but they would take their wages every week. As controllers of the temple market, Annas and Caiaphas raked in millions of shekels, determining the rate of exchange, till their avarice, corruption, and vicious luxury, their gluttony and oppression, were a byword among the people.[3] Again, it is no wonder that the indignation of Jesus was aroused against such evil, especially when that evil was carried on in the name of religion.

Let us try to imagine Annas and Caiaphas. We may think of them watching every movement that Jesus made, having their spies everywhere and forcing him to live the life of a hunted man for weeks together. The first preaching of repentance by the forerunner, John the Baptist, filled them both with hatred—the hatred of the ecclesiastic whose soul is

[3] Basil Mathews, *Life of Jesus,* p. 349.

dead, who welcomes no new movement in religion which does not emanate from the official class, and which, adding insult to injury, wins the people wholesale, though it lacks the authoritative backing of headquarters. Again and again we find emissaries of Caiaphas trying to trip up Jesus in his preaching, trying to find this excuse and that excuse for silencing him. "Whatever are we to do?" was a question early and probably repeatedly asked by the chief priests and Pharisees. "If we let him thus alone, all men will believe on him: and the Romans will come and take away both our place and our nation." [4] It was Caiaphas who hit on the crafty solution. Let him be handed over to Rome. In any case, the Jews could not finally dispatch him. They could label him as dangerous and put the onus of dealing with him on Rome, offering to their own Jewish people who adored him the answer that although Rome had martyred him it was "expedient for you that one man should die for the people, ... and not for the nation only, but that he might also gather together into one the children of God that are scattered abroad." [5] The cunning of it takes one's breath away. In one act they would destroy Jesus, put the blame on Rome, pretend to those who followed Jesus that Jesus was martyred by Rome and yet, by handing him over, pretend their own loyalty to Roman authority and

[4] John 11:48.
[5] John 11:50, 52.

their support of law and order. It is strange that in modern sermons we hear much of Peter's supposed denial and Judas' alleged wickedness, but little of the real villain in the Passion drama, who was undoubtedly Caiaphas. "From that day forth," says the Fourth Gospel, namely, the day when Caiaphas hit on this devilish plot, "they took counsel that they might put him to death." [6]

Imagine the feelings of Annas and Caiaphas when Jesus overthrew the tables of the money-changers, whose booths were popularly known as the booths of the sons of Annas. The atmosphere is tense with excitement. We can hear the muttered threats of the priestly party, the cowardly snarling of the money-changers, and the loud acclamations of those who were being fleeced every day as they changed their Roman money for temple coinage, when suddenly a voice rang out, majestic, compelling, vibrant with passion and challenge, "My house shall be called the house of prayer; but ye have made it a den of thieves." [7]

It is surprising that Caiaphas did not step in then. It was only his fear of the people, one presumes, that stayed his hand.[8] And when Jesus more and more asserted his Messiahship, it became more and more clear to Caiaphas that if he could make good his

[6] John 11:53.
[7] Matt. 21:13 (cf. Mark 11:15-19).
[8] Mark 11:18.

claim there would be small place for a high priest. What might have happened if Caiaphas had repented and had taken his official robes and laid them at the feet of Christ and asked him to take the office which was his right, no one can say. But wily ecclesiastics whose souls have been long since dead do not act thus.

The movement sweeps on in popularity in spite of all that Caiaphas can do, until it comes to the time of the great feast, and all Jerusalem is in an uproar, and stories of the magic power of Jesus are on every lip. It is believed that he can raise from the dead. It is said that he will declare himself at the Passover Feast. The spies of Caiaphas everywhere bring him messages that make even that cold-blooded snake feel nervous, and the impulsive act of Judas gives him his chance. Whatever happens he must get Jesus out of the way before the feast.

We see the marks of haste all through the narrative of the arrest and trial. Caiaphas is evidently afraid that Jesus, by his miraculous power, will outwit him. Judas had probably warned him that that is what Jesus would do. Judas may have told Caiaphas some of the things Jesus had done. Judas, as I think, had his own secret *hopes* of what Jesus would do. Caiaphas became more and more nervous. Why an arrest in the dark? Why a trial at night? Why were the witnesses not better prepared so that at least they would say the same thing? The court

itself went to the trouble of gathering witnesses, and
then their evidence was so valueless that the court
itself rejected it. Caiaphas was increasingly afraid
that Jesus would vindicate himself triumphantly. I
cannot help feeling that Judas deliberately increased
this fear in Caiaphas. "You try to take him and see
what happens. Do you think you can outwit a man
who can raise the dead?" If there is any clue here,
we can understand the haste of Caiaphas. Haste is
so often the child of fear. This must be the explanation of the arrest at such a difficult time, and the
haste shown. Though the trial is not as illegal as
we may have supposed, many illegal things were
done. It was illegal, for instance, for the temple
police to arrest Jesus. Jewish law demanded that a
guilty person should be both arrested and accused
by the witnesses against him. Further, it was illegal
to try a capital charge at night. It was illegal for
the judge to cross-examine the prisoner. It was
illegal to refrain from acquitting him when the witnesses disagreed. Further, witnesses proved to be
false should have been stoned.[9]

The charges that Caiaphas brought were: (1) that
Jesus threatened to destroy the temple; (2) that he
claimed to be the Son of God; and (3) that he stirred
up the people against Caesar. Caiaphas was not concerned about the third charge. He did not mind if

[9] F. Morison, *Who Moved the Stone?* p. 22. I am indebted,
in this chapter, to this thrilling book.

the people *were* stirred up against Caesar. Caesar would refer to him and perhaps defer to him. He could make capital out of such a situation. But he knew that the power of death had been taken out of his hands by Rome and that only the Roman governor could order the death sentence. So he had to include a charge which would affect Pilate.

That Jesus threatened to destroy the temple, Pilate knew to be a very serious charge in Jewish eyes. It was brought because it was a charge of sacrilege, and the leader of the Sanhedrin could ask the Roman governor to declare a death sentence if a charge of sacrilege were proved, though, since Pilate's power was not threatened, he might refuse to do anything. Further, it was devilishly clever for this reason: it had just one element of truth about it in that it was a travesty of something Jesus actually did say. Mark says, "There stood up certain, and bear false witness against him, saying, We heard him say, I will destroy this temple that is made with hands, and in three days I will build another made without hands." [10]

Of course everybody knows that it is easier to entangle a person by altering something he has said than to trump up a charge without foundation in anything he has said. The thing that troubled Caiaphas was the silence of Jesus, and we may notice that when all the charges had been made, the situation was hopelessly against Caiaphas. The witnesses

[10] Mark 14:57 ff.

did not agree among themselves, and the prisoner refused to say anything. Imaginatively we can enter into the feelings of Caiaphas. He had done already half a dozen illegal things to get Jesus there at some sort of trial, faced with some sort of charge. Time was terribly precious if he were going to get the plot completed and Jesus out of the way before the feast began—when he feared Jesus would vindicate himself as the Messiah—and yet at this late hour, after much precious time had been wasted, Jesus was unaccused in that the witnesses did not agree and no charge was definitely established. We may be sure that Joseph of Arimathea and Nicodemus, both members of the Sanhedrin and both friends of Jesus, if they were both present, made it as hard as possible for Caiaphas to prove any charges.

We now notice what the crafty Caiaphas does to break the silence of Jesus. Standing up in his place, dressed in the gorgeous robes of his high office, blue and purple, scarlet and gold, with onyx stones on each shoulder and jewels flashing from his breast, Caiaphas applied to Jesus the most solemn form of oath known to the Hebrew constitution,[11] the famous oath of the testimony. "I adjure thee by the living God, that thou tell us whether thou art the Christ, the Son of God." [12] When the question was put in that form, the loyal and truly law-abiding Jew had

[11] Morison, *op. cit.,* p. 37.
[12] Matt. 26:63.

no alternative but to answer. Jesus had always kept the law. He respected legal authority, and the law ran as follows: "If one shall say 'I adjure you by the Almighty . . . .' or by any of the divine titles, behold they are bound to answer." We have in our land and time nothing as compelling as this, not even to say, "Tell me on your honor as a gentleman."

The reply of Jesus was not evasive, though it sounds evasive in our translation. The three versions of his reply are as follows: "I am." [13] "Thou hast said." [14] "Ye say that I am." [15] The answer is the same. It was evidently made in what was a traditional, polite form to a question of grave or sad content in which courtesy forbade a direct yes or no. At any rate, in our speech, what happened was this. Caiaphas, in a way to which no true Jew could respond by silence, said, "Are you the Christ, the Son of God?" And Jesus said, "I am."

You can almost see the gleam of malicious triumph in the snaky eyes of Caiaphas as he swung round on the assembled rabbis, tearing his robe according to custom when blasphemy was spoken in the presence of a priest, and said, "What further need have we of witnesses?" [16] It looked, until the last minute, as though the whole trial were going against Caiaphas, but on the Prisoner's own admission, extorted

[13] Mark 14:62.
[14] Matt. 26:64.
[15] Luke 22:70.
[16] Mark 14:63; Luke 22:71.

under oath, the charge of blasphemy was established. As for the charge of stirring up the people against Caesar, we shall consider it when we are talking about Pilate.

Caiaphas had done enough to get the verdict of the Sanhedrin and to bring about the death of Christ. The Sanhedrin gave answer and said, "He is liable to be put to death." [17]   How easy it would be now for Caiaphas, the crafty, to whisper insidious things into the ear of Pilate to which he would be forced to listen! As Mr. Morison has said, "Caesar might be indifferent to the eccentric utterances of an itinerant preacher, but he could not be indifferent to a claimant for a throne. And Caiaphas had only to whisper this in his ear, 'If thou let this man go, thou art not Caesar's friend.' " [18]

It seems clear, probably, to many of us now that of all the personalities of the Passion who shared the dread responsibility of sending Jesus to the cross, the main guilt was the guilt of Caiaphas. We see in him a development that is almost terrifying. Here is a man who perhaps started his career full of idealism and hope—the high priest of God, the interpreter of God's mind and heart and will to the people; a man who should have called with the voice of a prophet, mobilizing the spiritual forces of that nation of religious geniuses against evil; a man not too im-

[17] Matt. 26:66.
[18] John 19:12.

mersed in organization to have a sensitive ear for
any voice in all the land that spoke with the accents
of heaven. Yet here is a man, possibly through the
influence of the wicked Annas, gradually becoming
the wily politician, the schemer for power, the victim
of covetousness and greed, until he becomes God's
high priest in nothing but name, and the incarnation
of those things in life which are fighting with dead-
liest enmity against God.

So when the voice of Christ was lifted up, calling
the whole nation to the highest, the voice of malice
and envy and greed drowned it with its own. When
eyes shone with love and compassion, with the flame
of a new spirit such as had never burned in the soul
of a man before, they were met only with the cold,
malicious glitter of hatred. And when hands were
lifted to heal and to bless, the hands of the high
priest took them and had them nailed to a cross.
The greatest enemy of Christianity was official
religion.

It will never be the same again. One cannot possibly imagine that official religion, at its worst, would
silence the voice of anyone who spoke the true accents
of God or hinder the hands of those who would
build the new Jerusalem. But the story of Caiaphas
points a warning finger in that direction. How
many potential leaders of religion in our land have
been lost because men who could have led became
officials and their souls perished within them? I am

not so afraid of those enemies of the church which we call worldliness, materialism, and agnosticism, as I am afraid of the enemies of God within the church.

No enemy is so deeply entrenched from the shafts of God as the man who has a counterfeit religion— the man who follows the custom, knows the jargon, engages in the practices of religion, but who knows no living source of power within the will, whose life has never been transformed, whose ears are no longer sensitive to the voice of Christ. He is the hardest person to win. That is why Jesus used spiritual dynamite to shell such men out of their dugouts and why he was gentle to prostitutes, for the former are in deeper dugouts than lust provides. Ecclesiasticism may be a more effective protection against the shafts of God. "The harlots," said Jesus to religious people, "go into the kingdom of God before you." [19]

So we may leave Caiaphas. We are not likely to meet him; and if there are those who are becoming like him, their path may not cross ours. But the lesson of the terrible depth to which Caiaphas sunk may yet remain with us. The spirit of Caiaphas is the spirit that has made the insincere ecclesiastic hated by the man in the street and made the profession of priest and minister looked upon with more suspicion than any other profession. Let us keep religion fresh and fragrant within us, never letting it sink to mere form and convention and custom. To

[19] Matt. 21:31.

do this, to keep the channels unblocked, to keep the springs pure and sparkling and unpolluted, there is only one way—to keep near to Him who can renew us day by day, and to whom religion was the sunniest, strongest, purest, loveliest, and most important thing in the world.

Chapter IV

HEROD

WE shall not be much helped by a study of this man's life, which might well become a history lesson with little religious significance. It is, however, of great interest to study his soul, especially in view of the part he played in the drama of the Cross.

He was not the Herod responsible for the massacre of the innocents. That was his father, Herod the Great, who murdered his wife and three of his sons.

The Herod we are studying, who, on his father's death, was given the tetrarchy of Galilee, comes vividly into the Gospel narrative through two incidents: his contact with John the Baptist, whom he murdered, and his interview with Jesus just before the crucifixion. The first incident is so revealing that we must look at it for a moment.

Herod was not an irreligious man; but, like so many of his kind, his religion was a weak sentimentality rather than a thing of earnest moral purpose. It is commonly supposed that he was unscrupulous, cruel, a murderer, a libertine. But in a true sense he was "religious." A psychologist would say that his religion moved him emotionally but not conatively. It was in the realm of feeling, but not

56

in the realm of will. He was a cultured man, artistic, highly strung, sensitive to the moving of the wind of the Spirit. As the grasses of the meadow are moved by the evening breeze but are in the same place, unchanged, the next morning, so Herod was swayed by the currents of religious thought about him; but no wind of the Spirit changed his nature or moved him to new heights of purpose.

Yet Herod could not dismiss religion as an idle fancy. It made him sufficiently uncomfortable to make him fear to be in opposition to it. He was very superstitious. For a time he thought Jesus was John the Baptist risen from the dead.

Probably Herod heard of the religious revival John had started. His arrest of John may have been prompted by a fear that John was about to lead a revolt. Certainly the people governed by Herod were in a state of unrest, and if Caesar in Rome heard of unrest on one of his frontiers it would not be well with Herod for long. But Herod may have sent for John. He may have thought how comforting it would be to his frightened conscience to have this man say that his immoral intrigue with Herodias, his brother Philip's wife, was all right—though if he did think this he was strangely ignorant of the result of his intrigue. For Herod, already married to the daughter of a powerful sheik, Aretas, had sent his Arab bride home to her father that he might seek to marry his brother's wife, whom he had met in

Rome. All the Arabs were furious at the insult; and since he had already lured Herodias away from Rome—from his own brother—to be his wife, pious Jewish opinion was shocked too. So both Arabs and Jews were hostile. And Herod had certainly mistaken John the Baptist, who was afraid of no one. "It is not lawful for thee to have her" [1] had been the blunt answer. Herod would have killed John had he dared, and Herodias continually nagged him to do it. But he feared the people.

Then comes the feast on his birthday. The scene is the grim castle of Machaerus, one of the most desolate places in the world, unbelievably sinister, built on the top of an isolated crag of black basalt 3,500 feet above the Dead Sea's eastern shore, with yawning precipices down to the water on three sides of it, and only a knife-edge of rock joining it to the coast. In the brilliantly lighted banqueting hall all Herod's company is gathered. The food is rich, the wine runs freely, and while they drink Salome, a girl of twenty, dances half-naked before them. Herod was notoriously lustful, perhaps hereditarily so, for his father had ten wives, nine at one time. Salome, in what was probably a "strip-tease feature," appears before him flaunting her physical charms to a sensual and sentimental man, gloating, lusting, and drinking alcohol which notoriously heightens sex desire and

[1] Matt. 14:4.

lowers the resistance of the will.[2] He calls her and offers her any present she cares to choose. She, put forward by her mother, throws herself half-naked on to Herod's knees, twines her arms about his neck, kisses the bloated face, and, whispering in his ear, asks the head of John the Baptist. And down in the dungeons of Machaerus, hewn out of the solid rock, the grim deed is done. "The king was grieved," says the First Gospel, "but for the sake of his oaths, and of them that sat at meat with him, he commanded it to be given. . . . . And his disciples came, and took up the corpse, and buried him; and they went and told Jesus." [3]

We know what Jesus thought of John. "Among them that are born of women there hath not risen [outside the sons of the new kingdom] a greater than John the Baptist." Yet he was murdered to please the spiteful malice of a royal adulteress.

The feelings of Jesus we have no right to guess. Some measure of their poignancy can be gathered from the fact that, as one Gospel tells us, Jesus im-

[2] "That a princess of the proud Herodian house should demean herself by dancing like a slave girl publicly in the presence of a half-intoxicated crowd of men is surprising, and it has been said that only those who have never seen an Oriental solo dance could regard it as credible; it is nevertheless not wholly incredible, however outrageous, to those who know anything of the morals of Oriental courts, or of Herod's family in particular. . . . . For a woman even to enter such an assembly was contrary to Oriental ideas of decency." Rawlinson, *op. cit.*, p. 82.

[3] Matt. 14:9, 12.

mediately said, "Come ye yourselves apart into a desert place, and rest a while." [4]   He needed time and rest and peace to adjust himself to the shock and horror of bereavement—time to battle with resentment against Herod and expel the revulsion from his breast.   Herod was the only man to whom Jesus ever referred by the name of an animal—"that fox" [5]— and is there no measure of the Master's feeling toward Herod in the fact that, while he spoke with Pilate, he was silent before Herod?   "He answered him nothing." [6]

Let us look at the other picture of Herod.   Pilate has sent Jesus to him.   Herod is not frightened now. The responsibility he will cunningly leave with Pilate. But he does want to see Jesus.   He is interested emotionally in religion and religious teachers.   So he is willing to "examine" Jesus.

Only Luke tells us of that mock examination. Herod wanted to see a miracle done [7]—note the superstition rising again—but there is no dignity or sincerity or moral earnestness in the situation.   Says Luke: "Herod with his soldiers set him at nought, and mocked him, and arraying him in gorgeous apparel sent him back to Pilate."   And Herod and

[4] Mark 6:31.
[5] Luke 13:32.
[6] Luke 23:9.
[7] Luke 23:8.

Pilate, formerly enemies, became friends over the body of Jesus.

I see in imagination Herod, with Christ before him, secretly feeling uncomfortable—as sensual people always do in the presence of real goodness; feeling, indeed, as if he is being judged by Christ—as indeed he is, and by the conscience of humanity forever afterward. I see Herod trying to break Christ's awful silence by his own derisive laughter and the jests of his soldiers. I see their bawdy jokes and innuendoes fall away from him. It must have been like watching the foul scum of a stagnant pool fall away from the unstainable white breast of a silent swan enthroned on waters whose filth she scarcely deigns to notice.

So Herod passes out of sight into another silence, the silence of death,

> Into that sad, obscure, sequestered state
> Where God unmakes, but to remake the soul
> He else made first in vain; which must not be.[8]

We cannot follow him further.

Look carefully at his personality. Highly born, good looking like all the Herods, cultured, fastidious, fond of good living, ready in many ways to serve the people, but overriding their deepest feelings to serve his own lusts, hopelessly weak, relying on craftiness rather than strength, religious only with a supersti-

[8] Robert Browning, *The Ring and the Book,* "Guido," 2130.

tious sentimentality, never with strong, dominating purpose, shallow-minded and cruel, artistic in a dilettante sort of fashion, the prey of his own morbid moods and fancies, a spineless worldling, lustful and sensual, the trifler—that was Herod. He trifled with life—he who could have done so much. He trifled with religion. He trifled with Jesus.

The two vivid scenes in the Gospels tell us all we need to know to appraise Herod's character. In the first he was frightened; so he sent for John the Baptist, hoping the Baptist would ease his conscience. When the voice of God spoke through John, he would not listen. His lust for Herodias beat too wildly in his blood. He imprisoned John, but the strange thing is that no one can imprison words. Once they were out of the prison of John's heart, Herod could imprison their speaker but not the words. They went on to haunt him day and night. Even when the voice was silent in death, the voices went on in Herod's brain,

Till a voice, as bad as Conscience, rang interminable
    changes . . . .
Day and night repeated: [9]

"It is not lawful for thee to have her."

Then we see him when he is not frightened, when Jesus is before him in Jerusalem, when Pilate has

[9] Rudyard Kipling, "The Explorer."

flattered him by an appearance of asking his opinion, when Herod is safe in his own palace with his toadying suite about him. And Jesus answered him nothing!

What would have been the good? Every reply would have caused only derisive laughter. Herod was not in the mood to listen.

As Herod passes off the stage of the Passion story, we watch a man going into a great darkness—who had been face to face with Jesus.

But can we leave the matter there? Can we look into the faces of modern men and women, and into our own hearts, and feel no challenge?

Every minister knows the people who come to church on a National Day of Prayer, a Harvest Festival, a wedding or funeral, a Sunday school anniversary, an Easter celebration, and are not seen again for many a month; or the people who come because they are frightened or want something, or the death of a dear one or some other seeming calamity is imminent and they rush to prayer like the mariners in Shakespeare's *Tempest:* "All lost! to prayers, to prayers!" And it seems to them that there is no answer. Do not denounce Herod. Look in a mirror.

All of use know those sentimental people whose religion is part of their culture but never part of their will, who can be made to feel emotionally but never to act sacrificially, who one day can sing hymns with gusto and the next defraud a customer. Do not denounce Herod—look in a mirror!

All of us know those highly sexed, unsatisfied, handsome men with whom no woman is safe, men who frequently make much of religious display [10] and think themselves broad-minded and artistic, but under cover of such labels indulge their lust on women whom they make their dupes—women who, themselves unsatisfied, fall victims to disarming words, seductive embraces, animal maulings, and often the marriage embrace itself. Look not back two thousand years, for it happens in offices and in fusty lodgings here in London; and while you watch in imagination Herod with a half-naked Salome, turn round and search your own heart for Herod's sins. Herod stole his brother's wife. Have you always been faithful, even in thought, to yours?

"That fox," Jesus called him. And we follow some of the treacherous cunning of the man, the cunning way he tried to insinuate himself into the good will of Caesar, building a town and calling it by the imperial name,[11] falling at last through his request for the royal title made at the instigation of Herodias. But before we have finished with Herod, let us ask ourselves whether all our ways in business

[10] Religious feeling and sexual feeling are dangerously close.

[11] The town of Tiberias was built by Herod on the site of a cemetery; consequently no one would live there. He had to subsidize Jews to open business in a place which for them was ceremonially unclean.

and private life are "on the straight," whether we would allow Jesus Christ to scrutinize our ledger, whether competition and ambition have never yielded to a single twist or deception. "Foxes" have not become extinct in two thousand years.

Superstitious, frightened, cowardly, cruel, cunning, deceitful, sentimentally religious in feeling, never religious in terms of purpose and will, sensual, lustful, immoral—Herod the fox! And Jesus, looking at him with eyes behind which the infinite but uncompromising love of God burned, said nothing. Nothing! It's a bad sign when Jesus says nothing. It means that a man is in a condition in which nothing can usefully be said.

Do you think that many were in this condition before the war? Healthy, prosperous, complacent, self-satisfied, prayerless, careless, smug, indifferent. And they said religion wasn't real and God did nothing. All the time Jesus watched them, but he said nothing. There was nothing to say. For the attitude of ninety per cent of the people in this country was this: "What need have I of thee?" Humanism —the philosophy that all man needs is man's efficiency—is one of the completely effective barriers to Christ. He answered him nothing.

> Just as I am, poor, wretched, blind;
> Sight, riches, healing of the mind—
> Yea, all I need, in Thee to find,
>   O Lamb of God, I come.

Yes, when a man cries thus, Jesus answers. But oh, my soul, bring not down upon thyself the silence of Jesus! "Unto thee will I cry, O Lord my rock; be not silent to me: lest, if thou be silent to me, I become like them that go down into the pit," into the final darkness, into the agelong night.

Chapter V

PILATE

As we try to look closely at those people who played a part in the dreadful drama of the crucifixion, I think we shall derive a twofold advantage. In their reactions to the events of the cross we shall see ourselves; and, as we gaze and meditate, there will stand out more closely for us the central figure of the Crucified.

Let us turn now to Pilate. He has little claim to greatness. He was not even a good governor. But, because he was the procurator of Judea at the most significant point in history, we do know a good deal about him, thanks to the records of secular historians, particularly Josephus.

We may think of a young man in his early thirties, about the same age as Jesus. A proud, hot-tempered autocrat of obstinate disposition, capable of childish behavior when anything thwarted his will, and as military-minded as his name suggests—"Pilatus" means "armed with a pike." Philo mentions "his corruptions, his acts of insolence, his rapine, his habits of insulting people, his cruelty, his murders, and his inhumanity," though some writers think this description exaggerated.

Pilate was appointed the procurator of Judea in

A.D. 26, three years before the crucifixion. His province included Samaria and Judea and extended south to Gaza and the Dead Sea.[1] His official residence was in Caesarea, but the possibility of riots in Jerusalem at times of festival, particularly the time of the Passover Feast, brought him to the capital. His rule over all in the province except Roman citizens was absolute. He had only recently, then, taken over the governorship, which was the crown of his ambition, and he was determined to show his mettle and keep the turbulent Jews in order.

Since it is true that one can never understand a married man without taking note of the wife he has married, we must look also at Claudia Procula. She was the granddaughter of Caesar Augustus and the illegitimate daughter of Claudia, the third wife of Tiberius Caesar. She was an aristocrat of the aristocrats, of royal blood, highly cultured, and, one imagines, sensitive to the religious and spiritual movements of her day. It may have been through her influence that Pilate was appointed to this coveted position.

It is strange to find her in Judea at all, since the law decreed that a procurator of Judea should not take his wife with him, partly because it was so dangerous, and partly on the same principle that prohibits a ship's captain from taking his wife on the bridge. However, princesses of royal blood

[1] Hastings, *Dictionary of Christ and the Gospels,* II, 364.

sometimes had ways of evading even Roman rules; and there she was, sharing her husband's life—a fact which shows courage on her side and devotion on both sides. Many wives would have been glad of an excuse to remain in Rome. Many husbands would be glad to be free. Perhaps she did not trust him out of her sight!

Let us look briefly at three happenings in the life of Pilate before he is presented to us in the Gospels. They will light up his character, and we shall be helped by them to understand his reactions to the Jews and to Jesus.

The first relates to Pilate's discovery that there was no image of the emperor in Jerusalem; indeed, that Jerusalem was the only city in the whole Roman Empire in which the image of the emperor was not set up, and before which the subject people did not bow down. Without asking any questions, or talking it over with his advisers, the new young ruler thought to make a great impression of his power by insisting that the images of the emperor should be taken into the Holy City.

He never made a greater mistake in his life. For a Roman who believed in a dozen gods to bow down to an emperor turned into a god meant little; but to people who believed that there was only one true God, and that to make any graven image whatsoever was contrary to God's proclaimed laws, the command to worship the image of a man was an outrage.

Pilate, incapable of understanding, regarded this as defiance; so he sent a strong guard with the images, and under cover of night these were set up on the tower of Antony overlooking the temple enclosure. It was a cunning device. The Jews were unlikely to demonstrate within the temple area, and if they attacked the tower of Antony that was an insurrection which could justly be punished by Roman force.

But Pilate was a baby in cunning compared with Caiaphas. The very next morning the Jews began to stream out, at Caiaphas' instructions, from Jerusalem toward the palace of Pilate at Caesarea. They gathered enthusiasts as they went, and several thousand of them—some say seven thousand—surrounded the palace of Pilate. They sent in their request to him to remove the images, but he refused. For six days and nights these thousands of Jews surrounded the palace praying, not to him, but to God to change the tyrant's heart. Every time Pilate put his nose outside his palace he was met with the spectacle of seven thousand praying Jews. After six days his nerve was broken and he told them to go to the market place, where he would come and speak to them. When he got there he ordered his soldiers to surround the market place, and spoke to the Jews from his tribunal. He told them that unless they stopped asking for the images to be removed and went home quietly, the whole lot would be massacred.

Many of his troops were Samaritans, who would have been glad enough to carve some fat Jewish necks with their swords. But the Jewish leaders showed an admirable spirit and a pacifism which was effective. They said, "It is better to die than to have images in Jerusalem," and they bared their necks and waited. But the word for massacre was never given. Pilate knew well enough that if one of his earliest deeds as governor was to massacre several thousand unarmed Jews, it would not be long before he was on his way back to Rome. To keep such a deed secret would be impossible. Caiaphas would see to that. So Pilate gave way and, with rage and humiliation in his heart, ordered the images to be removed.[2]

But he *hated* the Jews.

The second incident is not very dissimilar. Pilate wanted to supply Jerusalem with plenty of fresh water. It was a laudable scheme, and the Jews were as eager for it as Pilate. An aqueduct was constructed running from the pools of Solomon to the interior of the city. The difficulty was not the engineering but the finance. Pilate decided to raid the temple funds and to use money which was given for, and was always devoted exclusively to, religious purposes. Half a shekel, value more than a pound, was annually contributed compulsorily to the temple funds by every male adult in the community. As soon as the news spread that Pilate had burgled the

[2] Josephus vividly describes this incident in *The Jewish War*.

temple funds there was a rebellion against him, although he could not have got the money without the
connivance of Caiaphas, who must have warned
Pilate that a riot was imminent. Pilate tried to meet
this by sending soldiers disguised as civilians into the
mob, "not, indeed, to use their swords, but with their
staves to beat those who made the clamor. He then
gave the signal from his tribunal. Now the Jews
were so sadly beaten that many of them perished
as trodden to death by themselves; by which means
the multitude was astonished at the calamity of those
that were slain, and held their peace." [3] This was
met by a scathing rebuke from the emperor in Rome,
who was not slow to rebuke the governor who let
down the Roman tradition by having soldiers in
civilian dress using their staves on women. We can
imagine the sneering smile on the face of Caiaphas
when the two next met, for Caiaphas had probably
said to Pilate, "You have forced our hands in this
matter. We will pay the money under protest, but
we cannot answer for the people. There is sure to
be an uproar when news of this thing gets abroad." [4]

So Pilate *hated* the Jews.

A third incident shows us Pilate in Jerusalem stay-
ing at Herod's palace, as he did on festive occasions.

This white palace on a height near the Holy City
was a place of splendor hard to imagine. Halls of

[3] Josephus, *op. cit.*
[4] See F. Morison, *And Pilate Said* ——, p. 138.

marble contained pillars inlaid with gold and silver and adorned with precious stones. Three hundred guests could recline on couches and dine in one hall alone. The palace was surrounded by ornamental gardens with cascading waterfalls and beautiful fountains. Pilate, on one occasion, when taking up residence—and, of course, this was the only possible accommodation available for him in Jerusalem— brought with him a large number of shields bearing devices which belonged to his own heathen gods. Once more a report was sent to Caesar in Rome, who ordered Pilate to remove the offensive shields. Pilate gave way again.

But he *hated* the Jews.

There is a fourth picture to which, as far as I can discover, there is no reference in secular history. The only reference is in Luke's Gospel (13:1). Pilate had been responsible for the stabbing of Galileans in the very temple courts themselves and "mingling their blood with the sacrifices." This may have been some demonstration made by sympathizers with Jesus, Judas possibly among them, who made a demonstration against Rome, thinking to "hurry things up" and force the hand of Jesus, making him declare himself the Messiah in their sense and seize control of Jerusalem. It may have been the tense feeling in the city, disclosed in a similar incident, which explains the haste of Caiaphas and the nervousness of Pilate and their connivance in the crime

of plotting that Jesus should be done to death without
delay and certainly before feeling rose to its height
at the feast.[5]

In these pictures we see Pilate frightened, but
hating with a sullen and bitter hatred the people he
had come to rule.   We see a coarse, tactless, obstinate, bullying coward, fond of those blustering, loud-
voiced methods by which so often fear is cloaked,
and through which violence usurps the place of just
and legal authority.

With this picture of Pilate in our minds we can
look closely at the Gospel narrative.   Our view of
Pilate here is focused on the trial of Jesus; and, as
we read the story of that trial in the four Gospels,
there are many interesting questions we should like
to ask, and with which there is not space adequately
to deal.

Here are four questions which call for an answer:
  (1) Why was Pilate dressed and ready to receive Jesus and to try him at six o'clock on Good
Friday morning, the morning of the Passover,

---

[5] One authority holds that such incidents were common.   The
soldiers, told by John the Baptist to be "content with their
wages," could not, he thinks, have been Roman soldiers but
violent men, following Jesus in the hope of taking the Kingdom
of Heaven by force, *cf.* Luke 3:14 and Matt. 11:12.   Certainly
one of Jesus' followers in Gethsemane carried a sword, though
he seems to have had little skill in using it (Mark 14:47).   For
a full and excellent examination of these views see *And Pilate
Said* ——, p. 155 ff.

when, according to the law, because it was a day of the feast, no trial could legally take place?

(2) Why did Pilate say to Jesus, "Art thou the King of the Jews?" How did he know that that was the charge which was going to be brought against Jesus?

(3) Has anyone heard a greater travesty of justice than this, that when Pilate suggested that the Jews should try Jesus themselves, their answer was a refusal to try him *because they could not sentence him to death?* Can anyone imagine one of our courts refusing to try a prisoner, before the case had been examined, on the grounds that in the event of conviction the prisoner could not be hanged?

(4) What strange incidents lay behind Claudia's dream which impelled her to break the law herself by interrupting a judge after he had already begun to sit on a case; and further, can we account psychologically for the dream of the wife of a Roman governor about a wandering preacher of the peasant class? How the familiarity of the words of the Gospels blinds us to the dramatic nature of the events! Can we imagine the wife of a viceroy interrupting him in the middle of, say, an interview with a native preacher accused of making rebellion, in order to tell him of a dream she had had?

John Masefield's words express the situation;
Pilate is speaking:

Now, listen, wife: whatever dream befalls,
Never again send word to me in Court
To interrupt a case. The Jews made sport
Of what you dreamed and what you bade me fear
    about this Jesus man.[6]

Let us look at the last question first.

I am almost certain that there was a contact between Claudia, Pilate's wife, and Jesus. It may
have been that, carried through the city in her slave-
borne litter, she had seen Jesus, watched him healing,
heard him preach, even listened to his message.
Perhaps their eyes had met; sometimes, when the
contact is only a glance, very deep changes can occur.
It is not irreverent, I think, to recall and alter the
lines:

I did but see him passing by,
And yet I'll love him till I die.

It may have been that one of Claudia's slave
women, binding her mistress's hair or spraying her
with scent after her bath, talked to Claudia about
Jesus. It is possible that among her big staff of at-
tendants was some poor soul actually healed by Jesus.
It is one thing to be satisfied with religion when you

---

[6] "Good Friday," from *Good Friday and Other Poems.* Used
by permission of The Macmillan Co.

have all your friends around you. The gods of Rome were enough for Claudia in Rome. They gave little, but she demanded little. But now she was lonely and frightened. People need religion then. And in Judea the Roman gods meant nothing. What if this wandering Preacher who talked of love were right after all, and could give her that for which she hungered? Tradition tells us that Claudia was a secret proselyte to Judaism, that she was tired of the Roman Pantheon. Some traditions claim that she became a Christian.

It is certainly true that women are much more sensitive to new religious teaching than men. There must have been some kind of contact for such a vivid dream to have moved Claudia so deeply.

I entirely accept Mr. Frank Morison's suggestion that late on the Thursday night, when perhaps Pilate and Claudia were talking together in their cosy room in Herod's palace, there was a secret visit from Caiaphas. Caiaphas was compelled to make sure that the verdict next day would go against the Prisoner. He dared not risk Jesus being let off; so, I think, he called late at night at Pilate's lodging in Herod's palace at Jerusalem and made him promise that Jesus should be condemned. Tradition tells us that Pilate was up to the ears in debt to Caiaphas. If so, the latter would have a great hold on the governor, and one imagines that Caiaphas obtained Pilate's agreement that Jesus should be found guilty and condemned. This would explain Pilate's early readiness the following morning to receive a deputation and to try the Prisoner. It would explain how Pilate knew what the charge was going to be against Jesus. It would also explain the unworthy reference that the Jews could not try him because they could not put him to death.

Now imagine Pilate and Claudia sitting by the fire talking together after Caiaphas had left. They were lonely there in Jerusalem, far from their Roman friends. Their social contact with Herod was probably frigid and formal. Although Herod arranged for their stay in his palace, it is more than likely that during the feast he used another of his palaces and left Pilate and his suite as severely alone as he could. Pilate and Claudia, then, were in the house of one with whom Pilate had quarreled.[7] It is an uncomfortable, disquieting feeling to have to be the guest of a person you dislike and who dislikes you. On the night before the feast Pilate and Claudia were both nervous. They dreaded another riot. What would Rome do if another broke out? And Caiaphas hadn't given Pilate much comfort. Claudia wondered what the two men had talked about. How long do you think it would take a clever woman to get out of Pilate what had happened? Claudia, cultured and clever—Pilate, the uneducated ex-cavalry officer, bluff, rough-and-ready, hot-tempered, fright-

[7] Luke 23:12.

ened, and brainless! I should give her three minutes,
and I am sure that in that time she would succeed.
Pilate probably told her that Jesus was a political
prisoner of great importance who called himself a
king, and was likely to set up his throne in defiance
of Roman authority. Claudia gives her husband in
return a picture of Jesus which makes superstitious
Pilate shudder and tremble at the thought of condemning him unheard.

So we see in Pilate's mind a conflict raging.
Caiaphas is pulling one way, frightening Pilate with
stories of what will happen if Jesus is not destroyed.
Pilate is terrified that if Caiaphas sends another
report to Rome it will be the end of his governorship.
On the other hand, Claudia, his wife, whom he loves,
the royal princess with great influence, is pulling the
other way. She has terrified her husband's superstitious mind with stories of Christ's supernatural
power. Perhaps the interview was stormy enough
before they parted for the night. For hours Claudia
cannot sleep. She turns over in her mind all the
lovely, tender stories of Jesus that she has gathered.
Yet her last thought is that on the morrow her husband will—whatever the evidence—condemn Jesus to
death. It may be that to her Roman mind Jesus
seemed a god in man's disguise. It was a common
Roman idea that gods came down in the likeness of
men.[8] And his blood would be on Pilate's hands.

[8] Acts 14:11.

The conflict projects itself into a terrifying nightmare. In the early morning, though Pilate is already seated in the judgment seat, she sends him a message written hastily on a wax tablet, "Have thou nothing to do with that righteous man; for I have suffered many things this day in a dream because of him." [9]

Familiarity may have blunted our imagination, but it is almost an incredible happening for which we can find no parallel, and poor Pilate does not know what to do. He is even more superstitious than his wife. He believes in dreams as omens, portent messages from another world, but he is terrified of the fury of the Jews and has been miserably beaten every time he has opposed them. If he condemns Jesus, he is now superstitiously afraid that something terrible will happen to him. If he exonerates Jesus, he is terrified of what the Jews will do.

Now we must try to reconstruct the order of events. Jesus is to be brought from confinement in the house of Caiaphas to Pilate's palace. It is between six and seven in the morning. There is no one about. Matthew and Mark tell us that Pilate's first words were, "Art thou the King of the Jews?" But I think it is likely that Pilate would follow the course of the Roman law and ask for the accusation to be stated. This is what John tells us happened. "What accusation bring ye against this man?" But notice that all three Gospels fit in with our thought

[9] Matt. 27:19.

that Pilate knew already. Matthew and Mark state that Pilate said definitely, "Art thou the King of the Jews?" and John says that although Pilate said, "What accusation bring ye?" they did not tell him; they simply said, "If this man were not an evil-doer, we should not have delivered him up unto thee." (18:30.) They seem incensed that the plot already, from the first sentence, is not going as Caiaphas had arranged it should go. Pilate then takes Jesus into the palace to question him; and all four evangelists say that when Jesus was alone with Pilate, he made one attempt to get him to understand: "Sayest thou this of thyself or did others tell it thee concerning me?" Jesus wonders whether Pilate is really seeking to understand or whether he is taking part in a prearranged dialogue. "Am I a Jew?" says Pilate. "Thine own nation and the chief priests delivered thee unto me: what hast thou done?" To which Jesus answered sublimely, "My kingdom is not of this world: if my kingdom were of this world, then would my servants fight." Pilate, then, apparently asks him again, "Art thou a king then?" And Jesus answered, "Thou sayest that I am a king. To this end have I been born, and to this end am I come into the world, that I should bear witness unto the truth." And Pilate said unto him, "What is truth?" [10]

The accounts of the trial are harmonized if we

[10] John 18:37; cf. Luke 23:3; Mark 15:2; Matt. 27:11.

assume that in the presence of others Jesus answered nothing, but when alone with Pilate inside the palace he did answer every question Pilate asked. Pilate then goes out to the Jews and says, "I find no fault in him."

The trial is so fully described in all four Gospels that we need not follow the language word for word; but what I do think is of particular interest is to notice that Caiaphas had prepared Pilate and thought the trial would go straight through and the prisoner be condemned; then Claudia's message entirely upsets Pilate, so that we see him definitely trying not to have anything to do with it, not to undertake any responsibility.

Watch the evasions of Pilate. "Try him yourselves," he says to the Jews, and they make the reply we have noted, that they cannot ensure his death. Pilate tries again. "Send him to Herod," but Herod sends him back again. Pilate hits on the idea of substituting Barabbas, who, as we shall see, was not just a coarse highwayman, but an aristocrat, the son of a good family, a political leader. But the crowd wants Barabbas set free on the feast day and demands the death of Jesus. Pilate taunts them, "Shall I crucify your King?" But to that the priests have a reply ready that makes Pilate flinch, "We have no king but Caesar." The words go round and round poor Pilate's brain. "If thou release this man, thou art not Caesar's friend." So Pilate orders

Jesus to be scourged, and then weakly calls for water and washes his hands. How pitiful is his last attempt at evasion! "I am innocent of the blood of this righteous man; see ye to it." [11]

One last glimpse is given us. Pilate has one last kick at his enemies, an expression of the obstinate temper of a proud man, humiliated and defeated. He writes a title to be nailed up on the cross above the Master's head: "This is the King of the Jews." To designate a crucified person as their king is Pilate's last attempt to wound Jewish feelings. Again, like buzzing insects, the Jews annoy him. But like a sulking child who, unable to get his way in a major issue, stubbornly insists on getting it in a minor detail, the governor will not budge. "What I have written I have written."

Pilate threw a strange question over the balcony at the crowd. It is a question which has haunted men's minds ever since and which even now they cannot evade. "What shall I do then with Jesus?" What a strange and awesome thing it is that that is still a living and relevant question! Indeed, it becomes more relevant as day follows day. Pilate was only a poor, rough, frightened, blustering soldier, whose gods were Jupiter, Mercury, and Mars, and we are not to blame him overmuch in his terrible dilemma; for Jesus to him was a revolutionary, a poor Jewish teacher of no significance, with something so lovable

[11] Matt. 27:24.

that, after all, Pilate paid him a great tribute, "Behold, the man!" If Pilate lapsed then into his native Latin, a language in which there is no article, his words, *"Ecce homo,"* might just as truly be translated, "See, what a man!"

But the question is an even more significant one for us, for Jesus is not merely a man, but the one Hope of the world's salvation.

Evasion for us is harder than it was even for Pilate, for to the eternal question no mere historical answer will do, that Jesus was a Person who lived long years ago. No mere theological answer will do, that Jesus is believed by many to be divine. Some kind of practical answer is demanded from us. True, we may shut our minds for years against all thought of him; but in strange and mysterious ways he presents himself to us again and again, and we cannot escape his relentless pursuit, because somehow he has his secret allies in our own hearts.

There is a famous legend from which Mount Pilatus in Switzerland takes its name—that over the waters of the Lake of Lucerne at the foot of the Swiss mountain there can often be seen on moonlight nights the ghost of Pilate forever moaning, forever washing its hands. It is as though the whole universe will offer no retreat or rest to one who evades reality. And the fact of Jesus—his life, his death and resurrection, his teaching, his mission for the world—is the greatest fact with which the world has ever been confronted. We know that he has something to do with our inner, personal life, our business life, our social responsibilities, our national and international relationships. The only serious criticism ever really offered against the church is that it does not put him first, or show his spirit, or convince men of his relevance.

To react rightly to the story of Pilate is to face the fact of Christ. We wash our hands in the water of procrastination. "Not now," we say, "perhaps after the war." We wash our hands in idle excuses; in criticisms of the church and of Christian people whom we think do not very worthily represent him; in specious philosophies that offer comfort but evade his stern and relentless demands; in some clinging sin; even in some religious observance or social enthusiasm by which we offer him our service, hoping that he will not ask for ourselves. But he knows, and we know, that all this is really an attempt to evade One who can never finally be evaded.

In our heart of hearts we know that he is King. He asks for our complete and entire loyalty, because only so can he give himself completely to us.

As we bow before the Cross and feel, perhaps, the nearness of that loving heart, can we bring ourselves to enthrone him? If men would but enthrone him in their hearts there would be peace. Industrial tyrannies oppress men, but if he reigns, men will be brothers. Unemployment threatens some lives;

sweating degrades others; but if the Spirit of Christ were shed abroad in all hearts, we should find that there is enough for all to do and enough for all to eat. If we seek first his kingdom and his justice, all other things will be added. But what a big word is that little word "if." Men are selfish and unkind and suspicious. They trample on one another and exploit one another. "Myself," they say, or "my country," or "my interests"; and that Loving Spirit which alone can wield us all into one great fellowship is ignored or crucified. But we shall look on him whom we have pierced. However high we carry our heads, they will be bowed before him at last.

Evasion is really a form of crucifixion. I suppose we have always in our hearts condemned Pilate. But he was a conceited, frightened soldier, condemning One whom he never understood. This Jesus delivers himself eternally into our hands to love or to crucify, and *we* know that he is not a Jewish peasant but the Saviour of the world. What shall *we* do with Jesus, who is called Christ?

Chapter VI

BARABBAS

ALL four Gospels make reference to Barabbas.[1] Matthew and Mark tell us that the priests incited the multitude to choose Barabbas as the one who should be released by the act of clemency with which the government marked the day of Jewish festival.

It seems a strange choice. Mark and Luke say that Barabbas had committed murder. Luke calls him a murderer again in Acts 3:14. John says in four stark words, "Barabbas was a robber."

Deissmann, the great German scholar, makes it a still more dramatic choice. In the introduction to his book, *Mysterium Christi,* he says that the first name of Barabbas was Jesus; so that Pilate's question to the people was, "Which Jesus will you have, Jesus Barabbas or Jesus called the Christ?" Pilate clearly expected them to choose the latter. The people chose the former, but before we go further we must look at that word "robber." For, most assuredly, it does not mean either a burglar or a highwayman.

When Jesus said, "All that ever came before me are thieves and robbers," [2] he did not mean burglars

[1] Matt. 27:16; Mark 15:7; Luke 23:18; John 18:40.
[2] John 10:8.

or highwaymen or cutpurses. He meant that those who took the role of the Messiah in earlier days had been political revolutionaries, prepared to go to any lengths of violence and outrage to secure a political end.

From the Book of Acts we gather that such false "messiahs" were common. Gamaliel in his famous speech refers to those false "deliverers"; he mentions two by name—Theudas and Judas of Galilee—who "set out to be somebodies,"[3] but whose incitement to revolution came to nothing. And when Jesus distinguishes himself from others he is not calling *all* who came before him, including John the Baptist and the prophets, thieves and robbers. He is saying that those so-called messiahs who sought to deliver men were formerly political extremists intent on a political end. He was a good Shepherd, a spiritual Deliverer intent upon a spiritual end.

Barabbas was in the other category, as were the two "thieves" crucified with Jesus. Barabbas belonged to a political or politico-religious sect called the Zealots. They were banded together for insurrection at any chosen moment when the word might be given by their leaders. They were under a vow to murder anyone they came across who was taking good Jewish money from his countrymen and passing it over to Rome. Matthew, we may notice in passing, did this very thing, and later joined the band

[3] Acts 5:36-37.

of Jesus' followers. Then Simon, the Zealot, pledged to murder men like Matthew the tax-gatherer, became a disciple. Here is further evidence of the influence of the Master. It was the only thing that kept Simon's knife out of Matthew's heart.

Now Barabbas was a Zealot. As his name Bar-Abbas implies, he was the son of a "Father"; that is to say, he was the son of one of the official teachers of the Jewish law, a man who expounded the Scriptures, especially in their political implications, and who belonged to the religious aristocracy.

Barabbas had been trained in the traditions of Hebrew history and had been taught that to be a member of the commonwealth of Israel was the proudest privilege a man could enjoy. His childhood and youth had been spent amid the influences of a home whose chief interests were the things of God, whose dominating ambition was the steadfast advancement of his kingdom. He was a son of the manse who went wrong—as so many do! His heart burned at the stories of the glorious past of the people of God and kindled with a passionate indignation at the thought of the suppression of Israel. He was eager to share in any movement which would restore his people to the position of supremacy which all the prophets had told them was their inalienable right.

Think, then, not of a "robber" in our sense. No common criminal would have been put forward by *priests.* Think of a young Zealot with plenty of idealism in his make-up, real patriotic fervor, and a burning resentment against Rome in his heart. Then remember to make allowance for that deterioration of character which so often takes place in this type of man, whether in Palestine or elsewhere. What is idealism for one's own country becomes bitter hostility against another. Something good that is called "patriotism" becomes something bad that might be called fanatical "nationalism." Methods of violence and force speed up such deterioration; and, with Barabbas, the murder of the Romans or treacherous Jews became a greater motive than the dream of an ideal Israel. Probably Barabbas began his career believing that his cause was the cause of God. But, as is so often the case, it descended to methods of violence and plunder and robbery, spoiling the idealism of the beginning by the methods used to gain the end.

"Of all the teachings of history," says Lord Eustace Percy in his *Life of John Knox,* "the clearest is this: that those who seek to realize ideal aims by force are always unscrupulous and always cruel." [4]

In Russia one watched a program set out which seemed born of idealism and full of hope for a new world. The Russian program still has importance and value. The idealism is still alive. But visitors to Russia and students of the five-year plan agree

[4] P. 116.

that the means used have often been ruthless, and Christian values have been sacrificed to reach the end by as many short cuts as possible.

In India I have watched young men join Gandhi's movement, sharing his enthusiasm and idealism, and then lose the splendor of the latter in the violence of the former, bring the whole movement into disrepute, and cause their leader, the most Christian non-Christian in India, disappointment, sorrow, and vicarious fasting for their sins of extremism.

Would not one say of Cromwell that he stood first for a cause which might well be called "Puritanism"? But it was established by many a dark and bloody deed which sullied and tarnished its character.

Barabbas, no doubt, was a national hero; for if insurrection is dangerous in modern India, where Britain rules with such tolerance and punishes so mildly even those guilty of treason, insurrection in any part of the Roman Empire was put down ruthlessly, remorselessly, and pitilessly. Barabbas carried his life in his hands, and what a hero such a man can become who does that for a nationalist cause! Here is this daring adventurer who plunders under the very nose of Rome, who murders and gets away with it, who strikes in the dark against a great enemy. For a long time he escapes arrest. But two things are happening. No one can pursue the wild, reckless life in which crime dominates without that kind of life telling on character, however worthy the original motives may have been. And, secondly, no one can pursue that kind of life indefinitely. At some time or another such a man will make a slip, or somebody will betray him; and this, we may suppose, happened with Barabbas. Then the long hand of Rome stretched out, closed over him, and committed him to prison. And rightly—criminals must be restrained.

All this is so relevant to the modern situation which I want to discuss that I want to ask you to make the tremendous effort of imagining that you are in your early twenties, that you know nothing whatever of Christianity, that you have never been brought up in a Christian home, or lived in a country where the influence of Christ is interwoven with the very fabric of civilization. Then imagine that you are a young Jew, with keen, patriotic feelings, and before you there stand two men. One is gentle, very pale. He is weak and dropping with fatigue, for he has been up all night and passed through a mental agony in Gethsemane of which Barabbas is incapable. True, there is a majestic dignity about him, and rumor speaks of his healing hands, of kind eyes, of marvelous words. Rumor speaks also of utter courage of thought and speech and act in conflict with the proud dogmatic Pharisees. But is this, after all, the kind of leader that a young Jew with red blood in his veins desires to follow? Jesus has put his finger on the moral weakness of the Jewish religion, but he has dismissed as irrelevant the very popular desire to overthrow Rome. He is a Jew, and yet he is asking the Jews to love their enemies. He talks of going two miles with an insolent Roman soldier who asks you to go one, and of giving your jacket to the man who takes your overcoat from you. This is not the kind of leader, this is not the sort of Messiah who will deliver Israel.

Let the imagination next turn to Barabbas: manly, physically strong, with proud, flashing eyes; virile, undaunted; of the brigand type, it is true, but for that very reason the hero of the child mind, whether the child is grown up or not; daring, proud, the leader of many a risky expedition, the hero of a thousand escapades, the darling of the people, a Robin Hood of Israel who had taken his own life in his hand again and again for the cause they all had at heart. He is captured. Here is a chance to set him free. What matter if this pale, gentle Man who speaks so much about love be put to death? Barabbas surely is the synonym of leadership. Jesus, though very attractive to many, will get them nowhere. To stand up to Rome takes tougher qualities than Jesus seems to have—"Not this man, but Barabbas." One is not surprised that men shouted for Barabbas; most of them would do the same today. Few have been able to drag their minds away from that dearly-loved conception that leadership and power are something to do with physical strength and impressiveness.

Indeed, it was surely one of the temptations of

Jesus himself to take, to some extent, the way of a revolutionary, half religious, half political. If Jesus had lifted his finger, a thousand swords would have leaped from their scabbards and ten thousand voices hailed him as King. They were frequently trying to "take him by force and make him a king." [5] The devil showed him that with power like his all the people would rise and follow him. All the kingdoms of the known world might have fallen under his dominion. But he had put all that behind him. He knew he must not buy support by trading on nationalistic emotions. Besides, his vision out there in the desert was of a world kingdom, a kingdom which included even Rome. In that great heart there burned something greater than patriotism or even world domination. He could not be true to his vision and follow the path of Barabbas.

Now let us switch our minds from the first century to the twentieth. We may see in Hitler the modern Barabbas. We watched a country, sunk twenty years ago in defeatism and inferiority, become electrified by wild words, by bloody deeds, and marshaled by the biggest gangster in history to a military efficiency which has given it success in its brigandage in a dozen countries. We have seen the same deterioration as we saw in Barabbas. It was a worthy ideal to try to lift Germany from her spiritless defeatism, and it was expressed in many worthy ways within

[5] John 6:15.

Germany, but the methods used have damned the cause and its leader. World dominance has gone to his head. He succumbed to the temptation which Jesus resisted. He wants all the kingdoms of this world and their glory. And the end is for him madness, and for his cause failure, and for his followers and his victims an age of sorrow and pain. It so often happens thus. Patriotism becomes less a love of one's country and more a desire to dominate others. The pursuit of a worthy ideal is lost in hatred of those who seem to deny it. So the whole movement becomes a lawless and immense crime which, in the name of civilization, law, order, decency, and the highest values of men, must be put down.

But a searching thought remains for our contemplation. *The same government which restrained Barabbas crucified Christ.*

Our nation has dastardly criminals to deal with. Was ever a more fiendish act than Italy's waiting until France was beaten to her knees and then stabbing her in the back? Yes, there was one crime blacker than that. For an hour Italian airmen bombed a city newly stricken by earthquake and wounded and killed British rescuers while they were extricating the buried and tending the injured.

"The rise of the Nazis," says the Dean of St. Paul's, "resembles one of the less plausible thrillers. It was accompanied by gang warfare, intricate intrigues, conspiracies like the Reichstag fire, shootings like the massacre of Roehm and his fellows.   It has all the elements of a 'gangster' film."   There is no doubt that it is necessary to restrain such criminals, for the reign of law is the first condition of human well-being and a necessary condition for any possibility of progress.

But let us remember that however idealistic our cause, however justifiable it is to resort to methods of violence to restrain international criminals—and no other way would achieve that end—no nation can carry on a war like this without threat to its own soul.   Those who use violence find that it does something within them, blunts the fine edge of feeling, dulls the soul's sensitiveness, brings to birth in loving, gentle, and wholesome natures thoughts of bitterness, malice, and revenge.

I remember how a man who had been on the police force for forty years, dealing with the toughest and roughest, became a most useful church official.   But whenever we wanted to do something charitable, kindly, or tender, he seemed to think it was soft. His chin went out an inch or so and he thought someone was taking advantage of someone!   You cannot adopt, over a long period, the methods necessary to deal with gangsters without threat to the capacity to practice gentleness, humility, forbearance, pity, and love.

When the war is over a new war will begin, as

important as this—the inner war to purge our hearts of war's methods and war's effects on our own souls. For the new world will have no place for hate or violence. The values I see in Jesus are the values which remain, and to which, please God, the world will return when force and violence belong only to humanity's childish dreams.

Let us, then, be warned. Take Barabbas as the type of that lawless, treacherous violence which would seek to dominate the world and wade through seas of blood to do it. Take Christ as the Representative of those values of love, truth, beauty, unselfishness, freedom, and service which all of us in our best moments want to see disseminated and then established throughout the world. But let us remember that international justice is one thing—a good thing. Barabbas must be restrained. International revenge is another thing. It is a boomerang which returns to destroy those who use it. "Justice without force," said Pascal, "is without power. Force without justice is tyranny. We must therefore put together justice and force so that whatever is just is mighty, and whatever is mighty is just."

Let us soak ourselves in the spirit of Him whose world kingdom must be held together by love, justice, and truth, lest having won the war we lose the peace, and having restrained Barabbas we crucify Christ.

Chapter VII

SIMON OF CYRENE

W AS it a black man who carried the cross for
Jesus? "They compel one passing by, Simon of
Cyrene, coming from the country, the father of
Alexander and Rufus, to go with them, that he might
bear his cross." [1]   Simon may have been a wealthy
Jew who had migrated from Palestine to North
Africa, driven there by persecution, captivity, and
oppression, and who then came back to Jerusalem for
the Passover and who happened to be passing by.
If Simon were merely an emigrant, we have no
reason to suppose that he was black.

But a most intriguing situation calls for explanation.   Mark, whose Gospel was intended for the
Christians at Rome, specifically uses the phrase, "the
father of Alexander and Rufus."   This is a pointless
thing to say unless Alexander and Rufus were already well known by the time Mark's Gospel was
written.   Rufus we meet again, for he is mentioned
in the Epistle to the Romans.[2]   Simon we meet
again, for he is mentioned in the same verse with
Lucius of *Cyrene*.   The verse is most significant.
Luke says, "There were at Antioch, in the church

[1] Mark 15:21.
[2] Romans 16:13.

98

that was there, prophets and teachers, Barnabas, and Symeon that was called Niger, and Lucius of Cyrene." [3] Symeon is the same word as Simon, and Niger, as everyone knows, means black. So that we are entitled to read the verse to mean that there were at Antioch, Simon the nigger and Lucius (both) of Cyrene.

The evidence, of course, is not convincing; but, for my own part, I believe that an African played a part in the drama of the Passion. I think the evidence in favor of this suggestion is stronger than any that denies it.

Let us try to recapture the scene. Jesus is on his way from Pilate's palace to the hill of Calvary outside the city gates. He has been up all night. He has passed through an agony of spiritual struggle in the Garden of Gethsemane. He has sustained the shock of his disciples' cowardice and the strain of four trials, one before Annas, one before Caiaphas, one before Herod, and one before Pilate, with all that wounding to the spirit which comes from listening to false witnesses and crafty travesties of justice and of becoming the occasion of other men's sins. He has heard a mob cry, "Crucify." He has been subjected to the coarse brutality of a handful of Roman soldiers. He has been bound with thongs that bit into his flesh. He has been struck on the head till his head ached and throbbed. He has been crowned

[3] Acts 13:1.

with thorns. His back has been whipped with a leather scourge in the lash of which pieces of iron and lead had been tied, a punishment frequently causing death to the victim. Now they have placed on his raw and quivering shoulders two huge, rough beams of wood, under the weight of which he sways and staggers, fainting in the heat, and falling, at last, in all the filth and ordure of an Eastern street. This is the Christ of God, King of Kings, Lord of Lords, the only Ruler of Princes, to whom every knee shall bow. This is the one whose lips had spoken words of forgiveness and life, whose hands had been stretched out in healing and blessing, whose feet had walked on tireless errands of mercy and love, and whose very name for evermore will kindle new resolution and purpose in the minds and hearts of men.

The officer in charge of the soldiers moving slowly along the Via Dolorosa does not know what to do. A Roman soldier must not be asked to carry the wood for a criminal. No ordinary Jew in the crowd could be impressed into the Roman service. Our phrase "touch wood" goes back to the early days of Christianity when some of the devout possessed splinters of the cross of Christ and wore them as charms. To touch wood meant to remind oneself of Jesus and his cross. The best who wore such splinters would find courage in the touching. The superstitious would say it brought them luck, and the phrase has come down to us today. But when Jesus was carrying that wood along the streets of Jerusalem, no Jew would touch wood, for it would have made him ceremonially unclean to touch this instrument of torture imposed upon criminals by a pagan power. And if they were made ceremonially unclean then, they would be unable to cleanse themselves in time to eat of the Passover. What was the officer in charge of the party to do? Jesus obviously could carry his cross no further. No appeal to the priests was possible. Their reaction would most certainly be, "Can't Rome carry out its own executions?"

Simon solves the problem. As the little procession nears the gate to pass out on the way to the green hill beyond the city wall, the black Jew is coming in on business of his own—Simon of Cyrene, tall, strong, obviously not a townsman, and, as I believe, a negro. The officer in charge of the soldiers sees the solution at once. He would not dare to incur the enmity of the priests by making an orthodox white Jew unclean on the eve of the Passover; but, concerning a black man, white men have rarely been particular. So, in more senses than one, a black man carries the white man's burden. No one considered the feelings of Simon. Yet presumably he had come up for the Passover. One imagines that he was so devout a Jew that, whatever his negro name may have been, he had taken a Jewish name. At this time of high festival, his feet had turned toward the Holy City. Being black, he did not find it easy to get lodgings within the city and had been obliged to lodge outside. Every morning, however, he tramped into the city to take his part in the great festival, with buoyant heart and smiling eyes, with all his arrangements made to spend the day at the spot which, for the devout Jew, was the hub round which all the world revolved—the temple at Jerusalem.

Then the officer spots him. He looks strong. He is a stranger. He knows nothing of what has happened. If there is trouble through ceremonial defilement, the officer can say, "How was I to know that nigger was a Jew?" He will not command the sympathy of the people standing about. It is unlikely that his friends are near. The officer can compel him with impunity. So they force him to make himself ceremonially unclean and to carry a heavy cross, on a hot day, for an unknown Prisoner. In doing so, that rough soldier does Simon the greatest honor that could possibly come his way.

Simon did not know Jesus, and yet I feel that something happened on that walk. Between the gate of Jerusalem and the hilltop that we call Calvary, Simon of Cyrene came into contact with the most powerful transforming force in the world—the friendship of Jesus. It is incredible that Jesus would say nothing to one who, even under compulsion, was doing him a service. We do not know what was said, but even if the soldiers compelled silence and prohibited even the touch of Jesus' hand on Simon's shoulder, there would be some contact of spirit with spirit, for we do know that Simon became a Christian. Our evidence is that he is called the father of Alexander and Rufus, and those who received Mark's Gospel in Rome knew to which Simon reference was being made, for Alexander and Rufus were known to them all.

As one contemplates the part played by Simon in the drama of the Passion, there are three things that make one glad.

First, I am glad that Simon, the black man, is in the picture and that he recognized Jesus as Saviour, for Jesus belongs to all races. In a sense we might say that Jesus was a Jew, but that Christ is raceless. I remember a little girl in India who was shown a picture of our Lord which had been made in England; and when she saw it, to everybody's surprise, she cried. When asked why she was crying, she said, "I didn't think he was a bit like that." I think I know what the little maid meant. She meant that he was too English to belong to her. And when I think of the Christ who belongs to everybody, it seems to me as though every race in the world is engaged in painting his picture. We in the practical West can paint his hands. Africa can paint his shoulders. India, I think, must be responsible for his eyes. And the picture is not complete until every race has painted him as it sees him.

When we remember that we sometimes pretend that we cannot understand a person who is Irish—"Oh, he is Irish," we say—when we say of the Chinese that they are inscrutable, and when too often we excuse ourselves even from making an attempt to understand others because of a racial difference, it is more remarkable that Christ has been brought to every race under heaven, and they all claim him for their own. If Jesus was a Jew, as he was, it is the last thing that anyone remembers about him. "I have known him all my life," said an aged Hindu, hearing of Christ for the first time, "and now you have told me his name." A friend of mine in Africa, talking to simple native women, asked them what would happen if Christ in the flesh knocked at the door of one of their huts. "Would he understand you?" asked my friend. "Oh, yes," they said, "he would understand us. He would tell us what to do."

We may call Christianity the final religion, and so it is; but if so, we have not yet reached its final form, for to be a final religion it must include the truth in every religion. God has not left himself without witness in any, and the true Christianity is the final form of all. It will be something far bigger than the anemic thing we label Christianity in this elementary stage of the world's development. There is a place for black men in the picture, and red men and yellow men as well.

As I contemplate the drama of the Passion, I am

also glad to think that Simon gave strength to a fainting Christ. He bore the cross that could be borne by man, and so he helped Christ to bear the Cross that only he can bear. Christ's *body* failed, not his spirit. And so it is today. It is his body, the church, that fails, not his spirit. The body exists only because that spirit within it is deathless and divine. And whence will come the new life which that body needs? I believe increasingly that it will come from Africa and India and China and the uttermost parts of the earth. What if once more Simon of Cyrene, or the race which he typifies, gives strength to a Christ whose spirit is deathless, but whose body is borne down almost to the ground?

Here in our own beloved land we have a church at every corner. We have an immense and elaborate organization with a good deal of financial support. Books pour through the press which intellectually substantiate the Christian position. The church does not suffer from her doctrines not being expounded to the intelligentsia. There is much talk, though there is little witness.

But how weak the church is as an expression of the spirit of Christ. It is still his body, but it serves him in this country as a poor expression of his spirit, and it certainly does not carry his cross. If some of us were in India and had to live the life of an Indian villager and face the persecution and shame which Christians there face every day, our measure of

Christianity would be knocked out of us in a week.

The third point I want to make is that when they got to Calvary, Simon knew that it was worth while bearing the cross for Jesus. Those who have really heard him speak to them, or who have had him walk with them even for a few yards on the journey of life, those who have had a vision of what the Cross means and who have shared it with him, feel the honor of that sharing and know the joy of that communion, so that they never complain but feel humbly proud.

To be honest, I have never met anyone in this country who gives me the same certainty about that as some of my friends whom I knew in the East. I think of a young medical student who found Christ, as the saying is, in my old church in Madras. When he told his parents of his new and glorious religious experience, they threatened to end his career, to refuse to go on paying his fees at the university, and to turn him out of the house. He did ask me, rather timidly, in one conversation whether he could be secretly baptized until he was through his final examinations. Feeling very miserable, because my own Christianity had cost me nothing, I had to point out to him that baptism was a public confession of Christ, and the boy was baptized in a crowded church. Everything happened as he feared. His university career was ended. He was turned out of his own home. I lost sight of him for some months,

and then, when in 1922 I finally left India, he came
to the station at Madras to see me off.   With a
radiance about him that was wonderful to see, he
gripped my hand and said, "It was worth it, sir."

Nor shall I ever forget an incident that took place
on the desert in Mesopotamia when I was in charge
of a company of Indian soldiers camped on the left
bank of the Tigris.   A young Indian chaplain called
Subrahmanyam came out to speak to my men, who
were nominally Christians, a Christian company in a
Hindu regiment.   We drew two chairs out of my
tent and sat there in the moonlight talking, and I
asked him to tell me his story.   Briefly it was that,
as a young student in Madras, he had heard the call
of Christ while attending a Methodist church there
at which William Goudie was once the minister.   But
he came from a Brahmin family, and his father was
the head of the Brahmin community, and when
Subrahmanyam reported to his father what had
happened one might say that the whole village
blazed up in anger.   To try to make him change his
mind, they tied him to a pillar in the courtyard of
their house, stripped his turban from his head—
which is itself a mark of indignity in the East—
lashed his back with whips until the blood ran, and
left him standing hour after hour through the burning Indian noontide.   They even had the contents of
the sewage bin poured over his head.   He took my
finger in his hand and laid it upon two scars on his

cheeks where they had burned his face with red-hot
irons, threatening to put out his eyes. When the
men had done their worst and had gone off to the
temple, Subrahmanyam was subjected to another
kind of strain. His aged, white-haired mother came
out and pleaded with him as only a mother can.
"Subrah, Subrah," she called, using the shortened
form of his name as she had done when he was a
child, "I bore you, I brought you up, I love you.
You can't bring such pain and shame to me at the
end of my life." The boy tenderly answered her.
He had found one who loved him better than she did,
and he felt he must remain loyal to Christ. No one
seems to know quite what happened then. Whether
his mother took poison or not did not seem clear to
him. Knowing some experiences of Indian troops,
I find it easy to believe that she died of shock. At
any rate, his mother fell at his feet, and when she
was taken up, she was dead. Hearing a scream,
Subrahmanyam's sister rushed from the house. She
was only a child at the time. She cut his bonds, and
together they carried the body of the mother within
the home. Subrahmanyam made his escape to the
hills. But when the men came back from the temple,
they punished the little girl cruelly, and Subrahmanyam told me that she was kept prisoner for five years
for her offense.

I was glad it was dark out there in the desert, for
I could scarcely bear to hear this brave soul tell his

story, and he himself was almost exhausted in the telling. After he made his escape to the hills, he prepared himself for the Christian ministry, and was a Methodist minister who attained the highest honors of his church in India. But, honors apart, he too knew it was worth while. He was an outcast from his own people. Even if he tried to visit relatives long years after his conversion, they would not receive him. People I have met would call such a man a nigger, and some would put a derisive adjective before the noun. But there are few Christians in this country who are fit to touch his feet.

As we think of Simon, the cross-bearer, who carried the cross that man can carry, and as we think of Jesus, who carried the Cross that no one else can ever carry, let us dedicate ourselves to the task of bearing his reproach, even if that bearing interferes with our immediate pleasures and takes us out with Christ beyond the gate of comfort, beyond the walls of ease. Let us dedicate ourselves to the task of lifting others. Let us be willing, if need be, to go down with men into the hell they make for themselves and which others make for them, remembering that he has done this very thing for us—has done, indeed, far more than we shall ever know, something that must lie forever in the regions of impenetrable mystery.

'Tis mystery all! The Immortal dies!
Who can explore His strange design?
In vain the first-born seraph tries
To sound the depths of love divine!
'Tis mercy all! Let earth adore,
Let angel minds inquire no more.

But though there is mystery, there is peace.

"In the city of my birth, Benares," says Mr. T. S. Gregory, " a tribe of outcasts, bred in a tradition of crime for seven hundred years, became Christian. During the war they were lured to France by the promise of fabulous wages and employed there as scavengers. It was a strange land, a strange tongue. But one day they lighted on a Calvary. 'This,' they said, 'is ours.' " [4]   At last they felt at home beneath the Cross.

The true cross-bearer finds that in the shadow of that tall tree where Christ was homeless, all men are at home.

[4] *The Christian Faith To-day,* p. 145.

Chapter VIII

MARY THE MOTHER OF JESUS

No group of studies of the personalities connected with the Passion of Christ would be complete if Mary the Mother of Jesus were left out. Our Roman Catholic friends have emphasized her importance to an extent which for some of us does not carry our whole assent. They have deified her and made her an object of worship. Yet I am very sympathetic with them. They feel the universe ought to be a home. And what is a home without a mother? They feel that to call God Father is only half the truth. The other half could have been more completely revealed if the Jews had thought more of women. Jesus couldn't have told men to say, "Our mother who art in heaven," though it would have been just as true. But how could he, when every Jewish boy every morning thanked God he wasn't born a girl and was taught to do so by his mother? "Blessed art Thou, O Lord our God, King of the Universe," ran the prayer, "who hast not made me a woman." [1] Unable to call God "Mother," some men deified the mother of God's Son, and two popes later declared her "sinless." [2]

[1] Mishnah, Teah. chap. i.
[2] Catholic theologians claim that homage is paid to Mary but not worship. In popular practice, however, she is worshiped.

But even if we cannot go so far with them, we realize with awe and wonder something of the significance of the woman who gave birth to the Son of God, whose body was honored by his Incarnation. "That Incarnation," as Warburton Lewis pointed out, "began when Mary said, 'Into Thy hands I commend my body,' and ended when Jesus said, 'Into Thy hands I commend My spirit.'" Great poetry, great art, great literature, and great music have all paid tribute to the one who has been called the "Mother of God."

In our attempt to see her, however, I think it would be well reverently to put aside some of the conceptions which have appeared in pictures and in words, and to see a simple peasant girl, probably not more than fifteen or sixteen years of age, healthy, with rosy cheeks and hands rough and red from housework in a poor home, a girl of unsullied character, a girl of unwarped mind, unspoiled by over-fussing, unsophisticated in the ways of the world, unconfused by the quarreling of rabbis, a girl similar to the kind of fresh, virginal maiden whom one finds in one of our villages, one of the loveliest treasures in our national life. Notably, one imagines Mary to have been of exceptionally devout and receptive piety. No language could better express a complete and perfect readiness to do God's will than the matchless sentence, "Behold, the handmaid of the Lord; be it unto me according to thy word." [3]

Into the mystery of the Virgin Birth we will not now attempt to peer. Controversy has raged upon it and sometimes has almost seemed to sully the very thought of it with its wild vehemence. At any rate, Mary believed that her first Child was a holy person. So she

> With a sweet thanksgiving
>   Took in tranquillity what God might bring,
> Blessed Him and waited, and within her, living,
>   Felt the arousal of a Holy Thing.[4]

In the restrained pictures which the New Testament gives us, we watch her on that journey to Bethlehem before his birth, when one almost catches one's breath in wonder at the risks God took. For it seemed as though the salvation of the world depended on the stumbling footsteps of a donkey. We see her, after her terrible journey, giving birth to her Baby in the straw among the animals and laying him "in a manger." We see her, with eyes wide with terror, clutching her little one to her breast and hastening out of the jurisdiction of Herod. We glance at the lovely picture of his dedication; and all this time we feel we are watching a very beautiful,

[3] Luke 1:38; ἡ δούλη, translated by the beautiful word "handmaid," means literally "a woman slave."
[4] Myers, "St. Paul."

remarkable character, with a mysterious sense that to her is committed a very precious charge, and determined to discharge that responsibility fittingly and becomingly. Mother and Child are all in all to one another; and whatever her dreams and thoughts of her little one may have been, Mary is keeping them locked up in her heart.

Then there is that precious little cameo which only Luke gives of the visit to the temple when Jesus was twelve years old.[5] Here we have a boy who, because he is Eastern born, is even at twelve rapidly becoming a young man, eagerly sitting at the feet of the doctors of law, at the specified time in the temple when questions were allowed and readily answered. The boy is entranced with the whole subject that is being discussed. He is as interested in these things as some Western boys are in the inside of a motor car. We need not deduce any slackness on the part of his parents who missed him. The men would travel back together in one company and the women in a separate one. Joseph would think Jesus was with Mary. Mary would think he was with Joseph. When they met in the evening to partake of their meal and camp for the night, having done perhaps a quarter of their eighty-mile journey, Jesus could nowhere be found. How easily this could happen if we took a modern boy of twelve to the Motor Show, and someone was giving a demonstration of the

[5] Luke 2:41-50.

working of a high-powered racing car. Jesus was a human boy whose supreme interest was in the things of God, and he was so absorbed that the time passed without his noticing it. We can imagine the parents anxiously returning to Jerusalem seeking for him. But he had been well looked after; perhaps he slept in the temple itself, or perhaps some unknown mother had found him and tucked him up with her own boy for the night. In the morning he was back again among the doctors, with shining eyes and eager heart, keen on discovering as much as they could teach him. His mother was frightened rather than cross. "Son, why hast thou thus dealt with us? behold, thy father and I sought thee sorrowing." And he said unto them—if I may translate colloquially—"Why did you worry about me? Were you so surprised at my wanting to stay here in my Father's house?" Or perhaps even more colloquially, "I just could not drag myself away. I just had to listen to them talking about the 'things of my Father.' " [6] "They understood not the saying which he spake unto them."

We pass from these early pictures feeling that a shadow falls between the mother and her son, the shadow of misunderstanding. The words of the evangelist, "They understood not," [7] suggest diver-

[6] Luke 2:48-49. The phrase translated "in my Father's house" literally is "in the things of my Father."

[7] Luke 2:50.

gence.   The boy is growing up, and there is that inevitable breaking away of the child from the parents which causes so many mothers so much pain. But Jesus is also passing into a different phase of his life.   The spiritual world for him is becoming all-important, and the part he himself is going to play is gradually becoming revealed to him.   The words of Jesus suggest that such a misunderstanding as I have indicated clouded the happiness of his home life.   A person who was entirely happy in his home would scarcely have said, "A prophet is not without honor, save in his own country, and *in his own house.*" [8]   Or again, "A man's foes shall be they of his own household." [9]   "Thy mother and brethren stand without," they told him on one occasion.   They certainly were "without."   They were outside his circle, outside his followers, outside those who sympathized and listened and heeded and followed. Jesus stretched forth his hand—the only occasion when a gesture is mentioned—and pointing to the disciples said, "Behold, my mother and my brethren!   For whosoever shall do the will of God, the same is my brother, and sister, and *mother.*" [10]   And when a woman cried, "Blessed is the womb that bare thee, and the breasts which thou didst suck," he seems to have swung round on her with a rebuke, saying,

[8] Matt. 13 :57.
[9] Matt. 10 :36.
[10] Mark 3 :35.

"Yea rather, blessed are they that hear the word of God and keep it." [11] Gather together those four sayings and they do not reflect back to a happy home, but to one marred by misunderstanding. Those who are misunderstood at home are understood by Jesus. No one, said Jesus, who has broken away from his home ties for my sake shall lose his reward.

Jesus had five brothers and two sisters, so that, with Mary and himself, there were nine mouths to fill. We can imagine the little village home, and we can accept the tradition that Joseph died when Jesus was little more than a boy. It would be natural for the mother and the brothers to think that Jesus would take Joseph's place. They had no idea of the fire that was burning in his heart, getting daily brighter and hotter, a passionate longing to spread the good news of God's love through the world. To Mary and the elder brothers, here was a young upstart who wanted to preach, and who, when he did preach, upset ecclesiastical authority. In these days, in a simple home, a young carpenter who started out by putting bishops in their place would make his family look ridiculous in the eyes of the neighbors, and it surely would have been a miracle if Mary had not misunderstood her own Son.

It is possible that Mary thought him "queer" at the marriage in Cana, which may have been the marriage of one of Jesus' sisters. This would make

[11] Luke 11:27, 28.

Mary's importance at the festival understandable. For otherwise why should Mary be so concerned as to go to Jesus in distress and say, "They have no wine"? [12] We must not here discuss the miracle, but we note a strange reply even on the gentle lips of Jesus. "Woman, what have I to do with thee? mine hour is not yet come." The question is not as rough as it sounds. In Greek it literally is, "What to me and thee, woman?" It need not be any more rough than our English, "Never mind," or more colloquially our phrase, "What of it?" The strange word is, "Mine hour is not yet come." Surely Mary must have been very puzzled, but puzzled or not she has a very great respect for her Son. To the servants she said, "Whatsoever he saith unto you, do it." [13]

When he was crucified she was reconciled, and reconciled completely, and possibly this reconciliation took place long before his death; but probably she thought his death was a disgrace. One of the glorious things about Mary is that, thinking it was a disgrace and having suffered the sharp pangs of separation from him whom she had borne and whom she loved, she was there at the cross. As A. E. Whitham says, "The nails driven into His hands were driven through hers. The jar as the Cross dropped into its socket tore her nerves and wrenched her bones as the last travail pains when she gave

[12] John 2:3.
[13] John 2:5.

birth to Him, the thirst that inflamed His mouth scorched hers, as disheveled and worn, she watched Him there." [14]

Truly it had been prophesied, "a sword shall pierce through thine own soul," [15] but the most painful thing about that dread prophecy's fulfillment was that it was Jesus who held the sword.

As we look tenderly at the picture of the mother of Jesus, we surely feel that the world has done right to accord homage to Mary for at least four reasons.

1. She made a home for him.   First in her own body and then in the little house at Nazareth.   Modern psychology has emphasized, to a degree that is almost frightening to the parents of little children, the importance of the early atmosphere at home. Indeed, I always feel that Joseph's character must have been very wonderful, and I always feel a little sad that Mary should receive so much homage and Joseph be almost unnoticed.   For Jesus would never have taught the world to pray, "Our Father," if his own father had stood in a relationship to him which denied the love of God.   Beatrice in Shelley's play *The Cenci* had the thought of fatherhood spoiled for her, as has many another since.   But Joseph and Mary between them seem to have provided that unhectic atmosphere, calm, wise, loving, free, in which a little child's mind can grow up responsive to

[14] *The Indispensable Christ,* p. 124.
[15] Luke 2:35.

the touch of God and open like a flower in the sunshine. If, in the first ten years of his life, there had been quarreling in the home, or cruelty, or the things that crush and wound and distort a child's nature, what would have been the result upon the mind of one who was destined to become the Saviour of the world? Instead of that we read, "Jesus increased in wisdom and stature, and in favour with God and man." [16]

2. Mary loved Jesus from first to last. This may have been easy enough at first. I have heard many mothers say, when their children grew older, that they regarded the first months and even weeks of the child's life as the happiest for them because of the utter dependence of the child upon his mother, needing her, unable to do without her. But as Jesus grew up, there must have been occasions when his very development excluded her, when his plans and dreams and ambitions drove her into a hostility, even if it was successfully suppressed. One feels that the height of misunderstanding was reached when a voice, which may have been hers, said, "He is beside himself." [17] Yet one also feels that the bond of love was never broken.

3. Thirdly, she never attempted to dominate him. Here again we are beginning to learn through an imperfect psychological jargon the dangers of what

[16] Luke 2:52.
[17] Mark 3:21.

is called the mother-fixation, where a mother binds a child so closely to herself, binds its will to her own, excludes knowledge which might lead the child away from her, and establishes an emotional bond so strong that the child cannot—without a sense of guilt—be happy away from her and yet cannot be truly happy with her. He cannot, in fact, be himself. To be himself away from her would be not only—so he comes to feel—a species of disloyalty, but a sin. His animal spirits and instinctive tendencies have been misrepresented thus to him and labeled with that term, or its equivalent "naughtiness." So the child develops what the psychologist calls a "superego," the self he has been taught by close bondage to his mother he ought to be, a self imposed upon him through fear of his mother's displeasure. Since he cannot maintain this giddy height, conflicts which may later lead to breakdown are set up. The "id" or instinctive self is at war with the superego. In a forest when a sapling begins to grow too near an oak we have a similar thing. It cannot live either with or without the oak. It cannot live with it because the oak overspreads the very heavens and denies to the young growth below it the light and warmth of the sun, the strength of the wind to toughen its fibers and strengthen its roots, and the sustaining rain to make it grow. But then if the oak is blown over in a storm, or rent by lightning, the little sapling cannot stand the sudden demands made upon it. It has never been used to the wild ways of the world, and it perishes. One has seen so many lives broken by the selfish mother-fixations caused in early childhood, making sons very poor future husbands and daughters very imperfect wives, that one begins to realize all that Mary refrained from doing in regard to the precious life entrusted to her. There must have been times when she saw him developing along a line that was not the path of her wishes. Yet, as far as we can tell, she never thwarted his divine progress, pleaded his love for her as a reason for his doing her will, or repudiated him when he followed the path which he saw as the divine plan.

4. She maintained the family unity. When Jesus hung on the cross, he made provision for his mother. One feels that although he went his own way, he was always a member of the family, and a family cannot be held together unless a mother makes it possible. What is home without a mother? is really a very profound question, and the answer is that it is not a home at all. Nothing in the world—the friendship of others, earthly success and the applause of men—nothing on earth makes up for the withdrawal of love by a parent from the life of a child or young person. This is not the place to discuss the matter, but it is probable that every neurosis developed by a patient of either sex is due to the deprivation of love in childhood.

One of the things that makes one tremble in regard to the trend of modern life is that the home
seems to be disintegrating beneath our eyes.   Family life is the heart of national life and should be
the strength of individual life.   But even in some of
our so-called Christian homes, the house is a combi-
nation of dormitory and restaurant.   Young people
will sleep at home, since it is convenient and cheap
to do so, and for the same reason will take their
meals there; but they don't find their chief joys
there.   They don't find their greatest happiness in
being in what is sometimes cynically called "the
bosom of the family."   The members tolerate one
another, or perhaps do a little better than that and
have a friendship with one or more members of the
family, but the parents live in a completely different
world.   They sometimes heavily descend from their
plane of existence into the world of the children,
often only for disciplinary purposes, and then they
go back to live their own lives.   In those homes children really become separated from their parents' lives
at an early age, and those lives are never shared
again.

In a real home the joys of one are the joys of all,
the cares of one are the cares of all, the anxieties and
trials and difficulties of one belong to all, and, I
would say with deep earnestness, the sins of one are
the sins of all.   No discipline would be necessary if
that last point and all its implications were clearly

grasped. No youngster would continue in what is called sin if it were felt that that sin destroyed the happiness and harmony of the whole house and was a disgrace to a family every member of which truly loved every other member.

Christ's lovely vision of the world is that it is our Father's home. One is quite sure that his own home did not lack his loving support, and one feels also quite sure that the mother of Jesus maintained the family unity until the end. And no mother fails or misses God's plan who leaves behind her a real family.

One feels that even Jesus might have used the words of Kipling:

> If I were hanged on the highest hill,
>   Mother o' mine, O mother o' mine!
> I know whose love would follow me still,
>   Mother o' mine, O mother o' mine!

Her love did follow him to that high hill called Calvary. "There stood by the cross of Jesus his mother." [18]

We can afford a moment to watch her there. She is not old. She is between forty-nine and fifty probably. Her son is thirty-three. She was probably not more than seventeen when he was born. Yet she looks an old woman, standing there by the cross. The sword has indeed pierced her very soul. A

[18] John 19:25.

mother may misunderstand her son, but she will always love him, especially if he is suffering. Is it not her own body that hangs there on the tree, battered and mangled, bleeding and broken? Her mind goes back to his happy boyhood days in sunny Galilee. Joseph had been alive then. Life had seemed so wonderfully happy. And although Jesus was often in mischief, there was no malice in him. He was a grand Boy, so thoughtful and loving, so considerate of her and kind to the other children. She had prayed over his crib each night. She had mended his clothes and prepared his meals and made him wash his hands.

Then as a youth he had "got strange ideas," as a modern mother would say. He worked hard in the joiner's shop, it was true, but he would be out all night among the hills. He would talk for an hour at a time to the village rabbi, asking the queerest questions. Then he had begun to preach—and upset people, very nice, respectable people too. She had asked him repeatedly what he thought he was doing. When Joseph died, he was there to comfort her; but, as soon as his brother James could take charge, she could see that Jesus was longing to be off. Then came the day when he said, "Good-bye"; and the gulf widened till her stricken ears heard him say that those who did the will of God were his real relatives. How the sword was twisted in the wound that day!

She couldn't keep track of him, and at last she

heard he was going up to Jerusalem. She went too. His night of agony was more than any other could bear, but Mary didn't sleep all night. She knew, by the telepathy of love, that something was terribly wrong. Then she heard he was taken. After hours of terror and apprehension she "stood by the cross of Jesus." So it had come to this—all the things she had pondered in her own heart, all the bright dreams she had had and the visions she had seen when he drank at her breast and her fingers played with his curls. Poor little maiden-mother, what a strange, hard road you trod!

There she is now, trying to stifle her sobs, wringing her thin, toilworn hands, her poor dress stained and shabby, her lined face wet and white and drawn. Yet may we not in imagination see beauty there? And the beauty will shine out in a minute. For her Son is speaking. "When Jesus therefore saw his mother, and the disciple standing by whom he loved, he saith unto his mother, Woman, behold, thy son! Then saith he to the disciple, Behold, thy mother!" [19]

John's arm is round her. Her face, aged with sorrow, is lifted now. Jesus blesses her with his loving smile that makes everything right at last.

She passes from the Gospel story at its most poignant moment, but her passing is full of peace. Jesus' word and smile hushed her spirit in an ineffable calm. As quiet as still water is that bosom that has heaved

[19] John 19:26-27.

all day with sobs.   I think it is the word "home" that
gives us the feeling that all is well.   "The disciple
took her unto his own home."   And in three days,
sorrow will turn into joy and this dark night will be
followed by a dawn that will last forever.   "Hail
Mary! full of grace, the Lord is with thee and blessed
art thou among women."   On Easter Day I wonder
if Mary sang the Magnificat again, even if it were
softly, as if to herself:

> My soul doth magnify the Lord,
> And my spirit hath rejoiced in God my Saviour.
> For he hath looked upon the low estate of his hand-
> maid:
> For behold, from henceforth all generations shall
> call me blessed.
> For he that is mighty hath done to me great things;
> And holy is his name.

Chapter IX

LONGINUS—THE ROMAN CENTURION

THERE is a composition by Sibelius, "Valse Triste," where a mad dance of death, fast and wild and highly emotional, is sustained in the bass by a deep, repeated note which seems steadying and somehow reassuring. So it seems to me in the dreadful drama of the crucifixion there were weeping women, careless, gaping crowds "wagging their heads" [1] at him in mockery, derisive priests and scribes, a voice shouting, "He saved others; himself he cannot save," [2] mocking rulers yelling, "If thou art the King of the Jews, save thyself." [3] And one at least of the two thieves crucified with him "cast upon him the same reproach." [4] Then amid the hysterical taunts and bitter jeers in this mad and evil orgy of horror sounds a different note. "Truly this man was the Son of God," [5] or, as Luke has it, "Certainly this was a righteous man." [6]

[1] Matt. 27:39.
[2] Matt. 27:42; Mark 15:31; Luke 23:35.
[3] Luke 23:37.
[4] Matt. 27:44; Mark 15:32; Luke 23:40.
[5] Mark 15:39.
[6] Luke 23:47.

It is a Roman centurion, a member of the hated race of the oppressor, not even a Jew. Let us look more closely.

Roman centurions stand out very creditably in the New Testament narratives. One of them gave the Jews a synagogue at Capernaum. I have seen the ruins of it and the strange Roman carving on it which some think proves its authenticity. It is otherwise unaccountable, they say, to have Roman carving on a Jewish sacred building. Of that centurion Jesus said, when he healed his servant, "I have not found so great faith, no, not in Israel." [7] It is strange that at the supreme and solemn height of the Roman Catholic mass the words on the lips of the priest should be the words of a Roman centurion, "Lord, I am not worthy that thou shouldest come under my roof." [8]

Of Cornelius, another Roman centurion, it is written, "He was a just man, and one that feared God." [9] Of another, Julius, the centurion of Augustus' band, it was said that he "courteously entreated Paul, and gave him liberty." [10] And here is the fourth, standing by the cross and giving his testimony.

Some have written as if a centurion were a highly placed Roman officer. But a centurion was only

[7] Matt. 8:10.
[8] Matt. 8:8.
[9] Acts 10:22.
[10] Acts 27:3.

what we should call a noncommissioned officer. He was always promoted from the ranks and had under him only a hundred men, half the men under a British company sergeant major. There were sixty centurions in a legion. Strangely enough, classical writers tell us that centurions were laughed at as we laugh at sergeant majors for their pompous swagger and policemen for their alleged big feet. There is actually a reference in Juvenal to the centurions' fat calves and hobnailed boots! [11]

Some have written as though the words of the centurion at the cross were a confession of Christ's divinity. I doubt whether anyone in the whole Gospel story thought of Jesus as divine in our sense until after the Resurrection. One of the strongest evidences, to my mind, of Christ's divinity is the fact that in the first half of the first century the thought of that divinity found a home in the minds of Jews—unlike the Romans—who were monotheists to a man and in whom all their training and thinking was hostile to the thought of the divinity of a man.

Taking all the passages together, Matthew 27:54, Mark 15:39, and Luke 23:47, all we can say with certainty is that this rough and honest soldier, whom tradition names Longinus, paid to Jesus a tribute of admiration. This centurion had his ideals, common to most Roman soldiers. He knew a little about the Roman gods, Mars, Jupiter, and the rest. He had

[11] See H. V. Morton, *In the Steps of the Master*, p. 223.

been trained in the tradition of the Roman soldier, and he admired courage, valor, endurance, fortitude, and uncomplaining suffering.

Moreover, he had had opportunities of watching Jesus closely. If he was on guard over Jesus from the time of his trial before Pilate, he had seen a great deal. It is possible that he handed the message from Claudia, Pilate's wife, to Pilate. He may have witnessed the dreadful scourging and the crowning with thorns. He was in charge of the squad of soldiers in the procession along the Via Dolorosa when Jesus was bearing his cross. He marked his fall, his majestic mien, his uncomplaining, ungrumbling attitude. He heard the words of Jesus to the women, "Weep not for me." [12] He marked the attitude of Simon the cross-bearer and may have overheard a whispered conversation between Simon and Jesus. He noted that Simon never grumbled but carried the cross as though it were an honor, and only seemed sad that such an end was to come to such a man.

But the centurion saw more. He had no imagination perhaps, no sufficient sensitiveness to enter into the spiritual agony of Jesus. But a Roman centurion knew, and recognized, and admired above all things, physical courage. He had taken part in crucifixions before. He had seen Jewish prisoners shrieking in an agony akin to madness, going down on their knees to him, howling, whining for mercy, struggling

[12] Luke 23 :28.

madly with his soldiers, fighting to escape, biting at their captors, hurling curses at the indifferent guards. It had frequently taken half a dozen of his men to hold the prisoner to the cross while he was nailed there. Now he witnessed something without parallel in his experience.

The centurion's soldiers take Jesus and strip him. They lay his fair body on the larger beam and stretch out his arms on the crosspiece. They drive a great nail through one palm, a second through the other. The blood spurts out into the face of the executioner and on to his clothes, so that he swears. But there is no sound from Jesus, no resistance, no struggle. Only a great silence, broken perhaps by the sobbing of women and the cry of a vulture wheeling far up in the blue sky—and waiting. The soles of his feet are made flat against the main beam and a huge nail is driven through both. One dare not think of it for long or the sound of a hammer on big nails would become forever unbearable. The cross is lifted and dropped with its quivering burden into its socket so that, with the jolt and jarring, every nail wound would produce unimaginable torture as nerve and muscle were lacerated and torn to shreds.

> The creaking door of flesh rolls slowly back,
> Nerve by red nerve the links of living crack,
> Loosing the soul to tread another track.[13]

[13] John Masefield, "Good Friday," from *Good Friday and Other Poems*. Used by permission of The Macmillan Co.

Then began the long hours when his life blood dripped away. His head throbbed in the burning heat. Flies buzzed about his mouth and settled on his wounds. Through the heat haze his eyes rested on the fair city that cast him out to die. O Jerusalem, Jerusalem!

Even for the centurion it was a trying time, what with the heat and a storm brewing, though the Prisoner made it as easy for him as he could. Seven times he spoke—and what words they were. "Father, forgive them; for they know not what they do." [14] Turning to Dismas, on the cross next him, he said, "Verily I say unto thee, To-day shalt thou be with me in Paradise." [15]   In the midst of his agony he made provision for his mother and committed her to the care of John, "Woman, behold, thy son! . . . . Behold, thy mother!" [16]   Refusing all drugs, the myrrhed wine they offered him, he yet could express that awful craving of thirst.[17]   Then the mind wanders a little. The foam of delirium flecks his lips. As is so often the case in anguish that drives the mind to its own boundaries, he seeks succor where succor was found in earlier, happier days. Always the Psalms in the original Hebrew had comforted and inspired him. The twenty-second psalm glows with

[14] Luke 23:34.
[15] Luke 23:43.
[16] John 19:26-27.
[17] John 19:28.

the assurance of that final security which is his who does God's will. The psalm goes on to a tremendous affirmation of trust in God: "Ye that fear the Lord, praise him; all ye the seed of Jacob, glorify him; and stand in awe of him, all ye the seed of Israel. For he hath not despised nor abhorred the affliction of the afflicted; neither hath he hid his face from him; but when he cried unto him, he heard." [18]

Jesus begins to recite the psalm to himself. Below him on the ground the centurion catches only the first phrase, "Eloi, Eloi, lama sabachthani?" that is, "My God, my God, why hast thou forsaken me?" [19] Then the voice trails away into silence. So confused were the words that came now from the tortured lips that "some of them that stood by, when they heard it, said, Behold, he calleth Elijah." [20] This is evidence, if evidence were needed, that the words were not clearly heard. Thus has every minister who has watched by the dying heard the tired lips murmuring precious words that had brought comfort to the heart in earlier days. The centurion hears what only sounds like a cry of dereliction because it was an unfinished quotation, and he may have heard it through a storm which made even a loud voice indistinct. [21]

[18] Ps. 22:23.
[19] Matt. 27:46; Mark 15:34.
[20] Mark 15:35.
[21] Compare Matt. 27:46 and Mark 15:34 with Matt. 27:51-52.

No one knows where the spirit of Jesus went then. For a few moments at least he was beyond the pity of the soldiers, beyond the voice of Dismas, beyond the sympathy of Mary and the friendship of John, beyond the little group of those who stood there with bursting hearts. He was beyond Caiaphas and Herod and Pilate. They could not hurt him any more. And we cannot follow him any further even in imagination. The learned theologians are silent at last. The poor, simple-hearted centurion is left miles behind, far, far below. He reaches up and touches the Saviour's lips with a sponge soaked in vinegar and fixed to the end of a split reed. As if he is thanking the centurion for that last, kind act, and telling him that he needs no further human ministrations, Jesus quietly says, "It is finished." [22]

Through the storm clouds which had wrapped the scene in uncanny darkness for three hours[23] burst the sudden glory of the early afternoon sun. But the face of Jesus lit up with a glory which came from within. The delirium of torture was over. His mind cleared. His spirit exulted in ineffable rapture. His Father was *there*. All things were in his Father's hands. All things would be made clear. Every lovely value would be vindicated. His dying was not defeat, nor was he forsaken. God's inner word had been spoken to his well-beloved Son. The call came.

[22] John 19:30.
[23] Matt. 27:45; Mark 15:33; Luke 23:44.

The suffering in terms of a human body was over.
The fleshly prison prepared in the body of his mother
was done with. He was summoned now to the bosom
of the Father.

The end is not that of a criminal dying alone in the
dark. All three Synoptists comment on the "loud
voice" of his last words.[24] The utter gladness in his
voice startled all who heard it. It was the voice of a
Victor returning in triumph. As you read the Gospel
narrative you can almost hear the trumpets sounding
for him on the other side. "And when Jesus had
cried with a loud voice, he said, Father, into thy
hands I commend my spirit: and having said thus,
he gave up the ghost." "And when the centurion,
who stood by over against him, saw that he *so* gave
up the ghost, he said, Truly this man was the Son of
God."

Two lessons stand out for us here, I think.

1. The centurion's witness to Jesus was honestly
based on what he had himself experienced.

> What we have seen and heard
> With confidence we tell.

The trouble with a good many Christians is that they
tell what others are alleged to have seen and heard,
but which they themselves have never experienced.

Is there not a danger that we recite creeds and sing

[24] Matt. 27:50; Mark 15:37; Luke 23:46.

hymns as if we had been dropped down in the middle of a Christian experience, as it were by airplane? We expect our young people to "give their hearts to Christ" and "join the church"—and we are hurt and surprised and even annoyed when they don't—when they have never examined for *themselves* the evidence which lies behind our desire. Few can persuade themselves that something is true and worth while because others say it is so. Fewer can really embrace a faith that is so inexorable in its demands because it would please father and mother. Some sincere and splendid young people are as disdainful of churchgoers as the centurion probably was about the pious Jews and even Christians, *before he met Jesus.*

Is it not best that people should "look at Jesus"; that they should examine the four Gospels and read the lives of men like Schweitzer, Grenfell, Kagawa, Edward Wilson, Mary Slessor, until they begin to ask what power Christ has and is, so dynamically to change men's lives? Even if from a careful examination of the evidence a man emerged saying only, "Certainly this was a righteous man," it is an honest beginning and I feel that Christ would honor it. It would be better than trying to start where the creeds end with a pseudo experience for which the saints struggled for a lifetime, and then find in the hour of need that, though much was assented to, little was believed and no one was believed *in*. It is very sad to find a lifelong Christian and church-attender discovering in the hour of calamity that he has nothing of his own. He knows the language but not the experience. He goes through the forms but has not the fire of reality burning in his soul. Yes, there is something to be said for starting where the honest, simple soldier started. You may not get far but your experience is your own.

2. I would even urge that the second lesson we can learn from the centurion is to make our own "theory of the Atonement." This, of course, is not the place to record a dozen of such theories and try to appraise their merits. I left college in 1915 hungry to find a "theory" that satisfied me. Only within the last six or seven years have I been able to get the hang of an intellectual satisfaction about it. The theology of the Cross is mysterious, though the study of it is fascinating. But listen to the writer of a *Times* "leader." [25] "If the theology of the Cross is mysterious, the religion of the Cross is simple and convincing, having love as its source, self-surrender as its means, and the accomplishment of the Divine purpose as its goal."

That is a good place to begin. The centurion might even get as far as that as he meditated on the death of Christ. Here was a Man who loved. Love for him was everything—the dynamic of all action

[25] April 10, 1941.

and its goal.   Here was a Man who loved God and
believed that the thing that mattered most in the
world was to do the will of God whatever the cost,
leaving results in God's hands, a Man who sur-
rendered himself utterly to love.

Well, every man to the extent to which he is good,
is a revelation of God.   A perfect man is a perfect
revelation of God as far as man the vehicle can
express God at all.

If God is like Jesus, his love must be always
round about me, never leaving or forsaking me and
always longing to bring me into harmony with himself.   A love like that will stand by me to the end.
That's enough of a "theory of the Atonement" to
be going on with and enough to live by.   For to be
received into that love is to be saved, and to rest in
that love is to find the only security left in the world,
and to live a life that shows forth that love is to find
power and never-ending joy.

My mother loved Sankey's hymns.   Sometimes
she used to sing them as she went about her housework.   I think of her often, but I thought of her
vividly when I heard the Salvation Army singing the
other day :

> There is life for a look at the Crucified One,
> There is life at this moment for thee.

I wonder if the centurion found that day the beginning of new life within him.   It was a tremendous

thing for him to say, "Truly this was a good man."
Disciplined Roman centurions were not likely to be
heard publicly saying that a prisoner condemned and
sentenced by no less a person than Pilate was "the
Son of God" or "a righteous man."   It was a brave
act of witness, but it was rank insubordination, for
it implied a severe criticism of authority—the
sergeant major criticizing the act of the commander
in chief.   But Longinus could not keep it in.   Life
for a look! and life has a way of bursting the things
that try to hold it within too narrow bounds.   And
Longinus had only been looking for six or seven
hours.

> Life for a look!
> Look, look, look and live.
> There is life for a look at the Crucified One,
> There is life at this moment for thee.

Some of us have been looking for a long, long
time.   Yet how silent we remain!

Chapter X

DISMAS—THE CRUCIFIED
REVOLUTIONARY

JESUS was crucified on a Friday in April in the year A.D. 29, and we are told that he was crucified "between two thieves."[1] These two men have been called Dismas and Gesmas. The latter was the one who reproached Jesus: "Art not thou the Christ? save thyself and us."[2] The former, Dismas, whose name has the confirmation of the researches carried out by the late Dr. Rendel Harris, who was one of the greatest New Testament scholars in the world, rebuked Gesmas in a way that was very unusual: "Dost not thou fear God, seeing thou art in the same condemnation? And we indeed justly; for we receive the due reward of our deeds: but this man hath done nothing amiss."[3] Surely that is a very remarkable thing for one criminal to say to another—in one sentence to rebuke his fellow criminal for not fearing God, to acknowledge that he deserves the sentence, and to declare the innocence of Jesus.

But the mystery deepens. In the whole of the Gospel narratives there is no record, from the first

[1] Luke 23:33.
[2] Luke 23:39.
[3] Luke 23:40-41.

141

verse of Matthew to the last verse of John, of
anyone who spoke to the Master calling him simply
"Jesus." If the word "Jesus" is used, it is used in
conjunction with some other title—Jesus, thou son
of David,[4] or Jesus, Master.[5] They called him
Master and Lord. They called him Teacher and
Rabbi. Not even the closest disciples called him
Jesus. Yet in the last hour of his life on earth, in a
conversation reported only by Luke, who got it
presumably from Mary the mother or one of the
other women standing by the cross, we have one of
whom we have never before heard, who passes in
and out of the Passion narrative in a few verses,
speaking to the Master with unprecedented familiarity and intimacy, and taking part in a conversation, the implications of which take us into the very
depths of Christian thought. The Authorized
Version gives us the word "Lord," but the Revised
Version is not merely a better translation; it is a
translation of a better text. Luke, the doctor, takes
a pride in being exact. He says so in the first verse
of the Acts, and his profession would mean bringing
to his task a mind trained to observe and record
accurately. According to Luke, then, Dismas turned
to Jesus when both hung in agony on the cross and

----

[4] Mark 10:47.

[5] Luke 17:13. Note that Mark 1:24 is the word of a man
with an unclean spirit and that the text is confused: "What have
we to do with thee, thou Jesus of Nazareth? . . . . I know thee
who thou art, the Holy One of God." Cf. also Mark 5:7.

said, "Jesus, remember me when thou comest in thy kingdom." [6]

It seems to me certain, therefore, that Dismas had not only met Jesus before, but that he knew him well. The familiarity suggests that they may have been schoolmates. Certainly Dismas knew something of Jesus and of his intimate life. Otherwise what authority had he for saying "This man hath done nothing amiss"? It is certainly impossible to suppose that Dismas knew nothing of Jesus. He said, "Jesus, remember me when thou comest in thy kingdom." What kingdom? What did Dismas know of a kingdom? Why did he use the word that was on Jesus' lips every day? Had he been told, or even listened to, the message of Jesus about "the kingdom of heaven"? Had he turned away with an impatience similar to that of Judas and felt that Jesus' dream of a kingdom was too impracticable and would get nowhere?

Dismas is worthy of a long, close look. He has been referred to times without number as "The Penitent Thief." Actually there is no evidence that he was penitent and none that he was a thief. Let us look at the last point first.

The word used to describe both Dismas and Gesmas in the first two Gospels is the same word used

[6] Luke 23:42. I am indebted for some suggestions here to my friend F. Warburton Lewis, who wrote *Jesus of Galilee* and *Jesus, Saviour of Men.* See p. 182 of the latter volume.

about Barabbas in John's stark sentence, "Now Barabbas was a *robber*." [7]   As we said in the chapter on Barabbas, the word means a political revolutionary, not a burglar nor a brigand.

Dismas, no doubt, had done deeds of violence. He admits so much.   But they had not been motivated by personal crime but by national interest, a patriotism which had become a fanaticism.   They were aimed against Rome, not against society in general.   They were blows struck for a new régime. He shared, in a sense, the aim of Jesus to set up a new kingdom.

As to his being penitent, I suppose the many sermons based on this story that have been preached on last-minute repentance depend on the sentence attributed to Dismas, "we receive the due reward of our deeds"; but "deeds," we must note, is the word used, not sins. Where is the regret? Where is the sign of penitence? Mistaken zeal is indicated, or perhaps bad luck, but not "sin" in our sense. "Jesus, remember me when you come in [or into] your kingdom, for I was seeking the kingdom of God too."

Let us suppose that the familiarity Dismas shows

[7] John 18:40, "Ην δὲ ὁ Βαραββᾶς λῃστής. Luke in 23:39 uses κακούργων, malefactors, any kind of wrongdoer, but Matthew in 27:38 and 44 uses λῃσταί, so Mark in 15:27 and John 10:1 and 8. Prof. J. A. Findlay says: "Throughout the Passion Story thieves, malefactors and robbers do not mean highwaymen or brigands or pickpockets, but revolutionary extremists. Barabbas and the two 'thieves' were rebels against Roman authority."

is born of the fact that he was a former acquaintance of Jesus. Their roads separate. *Dismas seeks the kingdom through violence.* Indeed, from Rome's point of view, all three are seeking kingdoms other than Rome and are in "the same condemnation." If Dismas was a Zealot, as I think likely, he would claim to be seeking the kingdom of God. He takes the road Barabbas took, and the road which Judas, and probably Simon the Zealot, wanted Jesus to take. Dismas cannot hope to raise a revolt against Rome, but he passionately does what he can. He strikes here and stabs there and he waits. If a leader like Jesus had lifted voice and finger, Dismas and ten thousand like him would have responded in a revolt. But Jesus seemingly is content to preach here and heal there. Jesus will have nothing to do with physical violence and bloodshed and murder. Perhaps Dismas had been invited to join the disciples. Simon the Zealot was a member of the band. Perhaps Dismas had played with the thought of joining, but held back because he did not see how Jesus' movement could bring in the kingdom which, for Dismas, meant the overthrow of Rome.

Dismas listens again and again to his old school-mate. Jesus begins so many sentences with the phrase, "The kingdom of heaven is like." Dismas has heard the stories. Everyone is talking about them. Hundreds have seen him heal; others have been healed themselves. Hundreds believe he will set up the kingdom and prove himself the King. But Dismas just can't become his follower. He wants action. Where will Jesus and his men get with all their words? So Dismas goes on in his career of political agitator and revolutionary until one day the long arm of Rome stretches out, takes him, condemns him, crucifies him—and then on the cross next his own is Jesus and a notice over his head which reads, "This is the King of the Jews."

Something happens to Dismas. I would not call it a sudden repentance for sin. I would call it a sudden vision of reality—a vision that sees that violence and plotting and bloodshed can never usher in the realm of God. And it *is* the realm of God Dismas wants. He does fear God and believe in God.[8] Dismas is not the terribly wicked man of so many evangelical sermons. He is the deluded fanatic and agitator.

As Dismas hung there in agony that long, hot afternoon in "earthquake weather," as the sky got darker and darker and the thunderclouds piled up, may we not suppose that a revolution greater than Dismas had ever plotted or dreamed of took place in his own heart? It is possible that more words were exchanged between Jesus and Dismas than Luke records. We do not know. But one feels that clear as a lightning flash came the perception of Dismas that Jesus was right, that the kingdom he came to

[8] Luke 23:40.

declare was *the* kingdom of God, and, moreover, that though both were dying now, they might meet again in the kingdom of heaven—a kingdom that might be delayed on earth, but was real and eternal and accessible.

One is irresistibly reminded of some of Browning's lines:

I stood at Naples once, a night so dark
I could have scarce conjectured there was earth
Anywhere, sky or sea, or world at all:
But the night's black was burst through by a blaze—
Thunder struck blow on blow, earth groaned and
    bore,
Through her whole length of mountains visible:
There lay the city thick and plain with spires,
And, like a ghost disshrouded, white the sea.
So may the truth be flashed out by one blow,
And Guido see, one instant, and be saved.[9]

In that one instant while lightning flashed and thunder rolled and the earth rocked and shuddered, Dismas *saw*. In a hushed moment in that awful storm he turned his head, and his eyes met the eyes of Jesus. "Jesus," he whispered to his old schoolmate, "remember me when thou comest in thy kingdom." The Master smiled. "Truly, I say unto thee," he answered, "to-day thou shalt be with me in

[9] *The Ring and the Book,* "The Pope," III, 147.

Paradise." [10]   It was the Master's last interview on earth, and it remains the most glorious and the most amazing in the history of the world.

No mere criminal who did not know Jesus or what he had tried to do could have used the words of Dismas on the cross, rebuking another for not fearing God, expressing his own belief that death was not the end,[11] and pleading to be remembered.   It is right that the church should honor the great names of Peter and John and Andrew and the rest, but it needed the Resurrection to restore their faith.   The church should honor Dismas.   On the cross, in the place of failure and shame and pain, he believed in a kingdom that death could not end; and, to his everlasting honor, while the disciples were still in hiding, he believed that Jesus was its King.

What comfort does this lovely incident hold for us?

Let me briefly mention three.

Note first that the Gospel of Jesus is full of "thou" and "me," and when a man calls to him, "Jesus, remember *me*," that royal love, even though incarnate in a body tortured with an agony that for any of us would leave no room for thoughts of

[10] The Greek is unpunctuated.   Therefore the words may be read: Verily I say unto thee, To-day thou shalt be with me in Paradise, or, Verily I say unto thee to-day, Thou shalt be with me in Paradise (Luke 23:43).

[11] When *thou comest* in thy Kingdom.

others, cannot withhold a last sacrifice of self-giving. *"Thou* shalt be with *me* in Paradise."

In some moods it is hard to accept the thought that God can care for individuals. If we let the scientists talk to us too much about the comparative size of this planet in the amazing universe or series of universes of which they write and speak, we shall find this thought frozen out of our minds.

Indeed, if we let ourselves think of men at a football game, or crowds in great cities, or "China's teeming millions," or even a bus full of queer-looking people, we shall find it hard to believe that God loves the individual.

In the Old Testament, for the most part—with the exception of certain great psalms like the 139th—the matter is dismissed almost as ludicrous. The nations are only as "a drop in a bucket" and the "inhabitants of the earth are as grasshoppers."

But—and let me print this in capitals—IS IT LOGICAL TO DENY WHAT WE CANNOT IMAGINE?

All the logic is the other way. We must reason that if God loves the world at all, he can do so only by loving individuals; that if, as Jesus—the world's greatest authority on religion—taught, God is a Father, he will not forget one of his children. Logic would surely say that if God is really revealed in Jesus, then we must listen to and look at Jesus and we shall learn the nature of God. And if that be allowed, all we need follows. For he spoke of the one sheep lost as of concern to the shepherd, the one coin in the dust as giving distress to the owner, the hairs of our head being numbered, and our value far above that of the sparrows and that even they were dear to God.

We see a picture in the Gospels of a Man who picked out one verminous old beggar by a filthy pool; who gave the hot hours, when everyone in the East wants only to be let alone and to sleep, to a woman of doubtful reputation by a wellside; who talked with one troubled Pharisee on into the night. Jesus could not cry, "It is finished," until he had tried to win for his kingdom those who were crucified with him. And Jesus cried, "He that hath seen me hath seen the Father." So God is like that!

Indeed, any other alternative is rejected by this test. "Is this likely to be the truth?" Our reason answers Yes, for it is the highest we can think, and when we think about God we cannot think better than the truth. Nothing is too good to be true, though, as Dean Inge reminds us, "many things we want are not good enough to be true." "I will not believe," said Sir Oliver Lodge, "that it is given to man to have thoughts higher and nobler than the real truth of things." Any lower hypothesis we reject at once. In that case men fall like leaves from a tree to be trodden underfoot. Human life is only "a vapor that appeareth for a little while and then vanisheth away." Tennyson sings:

> Raving politics, never at rest—as this poor earth's
>   pale history runs—
> What is it all but a trouble of ants in the gleam of
>   a million million of suns? . . . .
> Stately purposes, valor in battle, glorious annals of
>   army and fleet,
> Death for the right cause, death for the wrong
>   cause, trumpets of victory, groans of defeat;
>   . . . .
> What is it all, if we all of us end but in being our
>   own corpse-coffins at last,
> Swallow'd in Vastness, lost in Silence, drown'd in
>   the deeps of a meaningless Past? [12]

Well, if life can be adequately described thus it is not worth living. It is a mockery and a farce, a bad joke, a fiendishly dirty trick, and the nature of God is not higher than that of the pagan deities who were supposed to make sport out of the lives of men. This cannot be true. Its alternative must be the truth: that God loves every man, woman, and child and has a plan for every life; and that finally, though evil can hinder and hurt, no soul will be lost. "They are mine," he says, "and they shall never perish, and no one shall pluck them out of my hand." A Jesus who will from the cross win Dismas means a God who cares for everyone.

[12] "Vastness."

The second thought that comforts me when I read again the story of Dismas is the certainty of Christ in regard to a life after death. I am not pressing more meaning into the word "Paradise" than it carried to the mind of Dismas. It may have been the only word about the afterlife that he would have understood. But it is as though he said, "I will meet you in the morning."

It so thrills me to realize the certainty in the sentence. Jesus didn't say, "Well, if we get through this . . . . if there is another life . . . ." He didn't say, "I hope we may meet again. I have faith in my survival and even in yours." He did not even say, "I can only be sure of immortality for those who believe in me."

Putting it at its lowest, what he did say is a remarkable assertion and the confidence of it steadies the heart. "A witness in his dying hour lies not." If there had been the shadow of uncertainty in the Master's mind, he would not have used such words to another, dying at his side. He who refused to have his body drugged would not seek to comfort another with a mental drug, to bolster up his courage with false hopes. I will not now enlarge on this point, for I have done that already,[18] but here for me is the strongest evidence in the world for survival, the survival of everyone. Here is the world's reli-

[18] *Why Do Men Suffer?* Chap. 12, "Is Death a Calamity?" p. 249.

gious Expert talking on his own subject. That puts
the matter at its lowest. Here is the Christ of God
revealing his Father. That puts it at its highest.
The Resurrection might be claimed only to prove
that a unique person can survive death. Here is
better evidence for you and me, evidence that life
goes on. For Jesus said to a political revolutionary,
"Today you shall be with me in the spirit world."
He would say as much to us. And who can believe
that Jesus would trade in facile optimism, false comfort, or easy, drugging lies?

One last thought. We are all like Dismas in one
way. We seek a kingdom. We fix our eyes on a
desirable object. In youth we would change the
world. But when the "forties" come, we look to
wealth, comfort, power, reputation—some self-bound
kingdom in which we shall rule in a little world of
our own.

Many slave all their lives that their children shall
enter a kingdom richer and happier than they themselves have ever known, only to find that their children grow up to take it all for granted and to show
no qualities of self-reliance or grit or sacrificing
service. Pleasure becomes their god and having a
good time their goal. The least hardship draws a
grumble from them. All the struggle of their parents has brought the kingdom of heaven no nearer
for them or for anyone else.

It would be good to think that anyone who reads

this chapter would sit back and say, "I, too, seek a kingdom. What is it that I seek?"

There is a kingdom of right relationships which Jesus called the Kingdom of Heaven, where men look up into the face of God and say, "Father," and into the faces of men and women and say, "My brothers and sisters"; where unselfish service is the key to happiness and where the reward is the exquisite joy of being one with God because one is trying above all things to do his will.

Dismas followed the wrong lights all his life, and then suddenly on the cross he saw the way and followed it. How sad that it was so late before he found out the way! For one of the saddest things in the world is to spend all your life trying to realize an ambition, and to find when you reach it that it has nothing in it to give you final satisfaction or deep contentment, so that, late in the day, tired, and with the sun declining, you must pick up your luggage and look for another road.

So many are so near to *the* kingdom. The picture in my mind is that of a young man in a fine automobile full of gasoline, the car in splendid order. All could be so glorious, and he could give so many people lifts on the way. And he pulls up where the road forks. You watch and wait breathlessly—then to your dismay he takes the wrong fork. You call after him, but he cannot hear. He drives fast, and the road brings him out to what seems like pleasure and feels like success and looks like happiness; but you know—perhaps through your own bitter experience—that the road goes nowhere, ends in a precipice, and that those who go along it either turn back or. . . . .

Don't follow Dismas and turn back at the last milestone. Seek God's kingdom now, with all the kingdoms of the world in sight. He leans out of his immensity, loving *you* amid all earth's millions, wanting *you,* calling *you,* pleading with *you,* and offering you your place in his plan.

He longs for as personal a response, not your anemic following at the far edge of the crowd, or your support of his work, or your languid and distant admiration, but the full loyalty and utter lifelong devotion of one who looks into his face and cries, "My Lord, My God." You could enter his kingdom *now.*

Chapter XI

JOSEPH OF ARIMATHEA

PROBABLY Joseph of Arimathea was the only unhappy man among all Jesus' followers on Easter morning. What a morning of joy it was! I know nothing in literature or poetry or art which quite conveys the feeling tone of that morning. Words cannot do it. Music would come nearest. But there are some words we can say over to ourselves, words which kindle a mental atmosphere that helps us. Spring, dawn, bird song, the tree-shadowed garden, the dew-drenched grass. Then the sun! The long shadows over the grass. The women with their spices coming to do the last offices. The exultant young man in the tomb. The race of Peter and John. Mary weeping. The Gardener—his self-revelation through the way he called her name in that thrilling voice—"Mary!" And the one-word response for which we need four. "Rabboni"—"O my great Master." [1]

The utter beauty and rightness of it! The triumph of it! The joy which cries for utter gladness! He is risen! Three words, the joy of which we cannot imagine; the nearest we can imagine will be three

[1] John 20:16.

156

more words—and may they come soon—"war is over"; or three more—"we have won!"

What a morning!—a morning which accounts for tens of thousands of people singing every Easter day, with a joy that would defy analysis, the words, "Jesus Christ is risen today, Alleluia!"—a joy that has come down the ages so that in the darkest days of war, if we let our minds turn to Easter, we find a new spring in our step, a new courage and hope in our hearts, because we know that goodness and sacrifice cannot be crushed by evil. I like to let my mind run across the world on Easter morning— Africans in tiny villages, Indians in the jungle clearings, Chinese in swarming cities, Eskimos in the frozen north, South Sea Islanders in blazing sunshine, all singing, singing, singing, because nineteen hundred years ago in the garden of Joseph of Arimathea the Christ of God, crucified by evil, was raised up by the power of God. It is good, too, on Easter morning to think of the glorious enterprises springing out of Easter. In ten thousand hospitals and schools and colleges and churches and homes, on the high seas, in scorching deserts and arctic wastes, nothing that war with its violence and oppression and tyranny and pain and sorrow can do will prevent men's hearts from rising in joy unquenchable. They know that love conquers death, that goodness is invulnerable, that God is in heaven and the dark night of evil must pass.

Ah! Joseph, you made a garden, and in that garden was your own tomb. It would have been a garden of sorrowful remembrance. But you brought to it one whom death could not hold. Your garden held the hopes of all the world. More has grown from your garden than you dreamed. Hope and faith and courage and joy have flourished all over the world from that frail, broken body sown in your garden on the darkest night the world has known and raised in splendor on the first day of a New Age.

But on that first morning I think Joseph was unhappy—Joseph of Arimathea, the little hill town in which the prophet Samuel was born. Not that Joseph was a bad man. On the contrary, we are told many creditable things about him. He wrought a great service to every lover of Jesus, since, but for his offering of his own tomb, the body of Jesus would have been flung out on to the refuse heaps in the valley of Gehenna. He bought the body of Jesus from Pilate. That took courage, and it cost him more than thirty pieces of silver. In the eyes of the law he defiled his own tomb by placing in it the body of Jesus. He was, we learn, a councilor, a good man and righteous. He had not consented to Christ's death. He was looking for the kingdom of God. He was a disciple of Jesus—but secretly, for fear.[2]

Have you ever tried to enter into the feelings of one, in the hour of the triumph of some cause, who

[2] John 19:38.

has only halfheartedly supported that cause? Have
you ever known a schoolmaster withhold encouragement from a pupil, give him only grudging support,
warn him repeatedly of failure when perhaps another
master gives every possible and open support? The
pupil comes through the ordeal with flying colors.
The latter says, "Well done! I told you so. Splendid!" The former is almost shamefaced, "Well, to
tell you the truth, Jones, I didn't think you had it
in you."

Some words of Dr. Hutton written in another con-
nection strike the note I want to sound:

> I do not know a man who has so definitely de-
> prived himself of a source of happiness later on,
> when our sources are apt to fail, as is the man who
> knows that once upon a time he might have done a
> fine thing, a thing that would perhaps have crucified
> his natural inclination, but would have made a man
> of him—and he did not do it. The awful retribution
> awaiting such a man is that one day he has to look at
> the thing done, accomplished, built—without him.
> I do not envy any man who stood out when a big
> thing was on hand, and one day the big thing wins
> the day, and he had never shed a drop of his blood
> for it. Do you wonder that later a man like that will
> go and beseech some power, or someone, to give him
> *now* a moral task which shall prove to himself that
> he is still a man, he himself having proved on a
> former occasion that he was no man at all? For
> what is the definition of a man, except that he is that
> being of all God's creatures who for the sake of a

moral idea can trample upon his own sense of comfort? I know of no other valid definition of a man.[8]

I only use this to get an angle on Joseph of Arimathea's attitude to Jesus. Of course, full and loyal support wasn't easy. Joseph was a Jewish councilor, a member of the Sanhedrin. Had it been known that he was a disciple of Jesus, he would not only have been turned out of the Sanhedrin, but denied the fellowship of even the synagogue. It wasn't so easy for him as it was for a Jewish fisherman. He had what the Chinese call "face" to save. He was a "big pot." True, he waited for the kingdom of God, but he didn't mean what we mean. He meant a move to displace Rome. He had to be very careful. He wasn't quite sure that Jesus was going to do that. He felt he mustn't be rushed into supporting him. He was attracted by his teaching, fascinated by his miracles, charmed by the spell of his personality. He had not consented to his death. He had offered his own tomb for the burial.

> He bears Him to his new wrought tomb,
>   Jesus, to whom he would not bow.
> He leaves Him in its sacred gloom,
>   His Lord and Saviour—now.

Ah, yes, but even now, not openly, for fear of the Jews.

[8] *British Weekly,* April 17, 1941.

Then came that dawn! If only he had given wholehearted support to Jesus in the day of his greatest need, if he had stood by Jesus at all costs, hauled his flag to the masthead and nailed his colors there, what inward joy would have been his on the day of resurrection! If only he had realized that a tiny bunch of flowers to the living is worth a dozen wreaths to the dead.

But, though the evangelists speak of him kindly, we see in Joseph just the weakness of those lovable people who could do so much and yet who do so little. "He *waited* for the kingdom of God," they said. And no kingdom is brought in thus, least of all God's. He was a disciple, but secretly for fear!

There is another touch in the Gospel portrait that points to his weakness of character. Mark says about the trial before the Sanhedrin, "They *all* condemned him to be liable to death." [4] Luke says that Joseph "had not consented to their counsel and deed." [5] Probably the two statements can be harmonized by the obvious inference that Joseph did not vote against the Sanhedrin's resolution and yet did not consent to the death of Jesus, because he was not there. When, in the night, the messenger came summoning him to attend, he just didn't go! He stayed in bed. I wonder if his wife said, "Don't go, Joseph, you'll only make your cold worse." After

[4] Mark 14:64.
[5] Luke 23:51.

all, it was illegal, anyway, thought Joseph, to summon the Sanhedrin in the dead of night. He turned over and went to sleep. He would make some inquiries in the morning.

We hear little more of Joseph. He was probably thrown out of the Sanhedrin, but we never hear that he allied himself with the infant church. It would have been better, if he *had* to go down, to have done so with all the bands playing and flags flying. Instead, battered in the mental conflict, he seems to have stolen away in the dusk, with bands muted and flags hauled down. We never hear his name again, either in the Sanhedrin or in the church. Yet the Sanhedrin is mentioned over and over again. Distinguished people in it, friendly to Christianity like Gamaliel, are named. And had he, in the church, exerted a great influence, we should probably have encountered him. Luke speaks kindly of Joseph in the Gospel, but he never mentions him in the Acts.

I fear it is only an interesting legend that Joseph was imprisoned, and then released by further payment to Pilate; that he became the possessor of the Holy Grail and was sent by the Apostle Philip to England; that he found, in the swamps of Somerset, a mound reminding him of Mount Tabor; that he kept the Grail there and built the first Christian sanctuary in these islands in A.D. 63 at Glastonbury, where a great abbey—the ruins of which can still be seen—was built. There may be a measure of truth behind these stories, but the age of Joseph would seem to make the details impossible.

There is a message for us today from our study of Joseph. Let me set it down in the form of four beatitudes.

1. *Blessed are they who at midnight are sure of the dawn.*

Some of us know what that means in personal lives. It is easy to support with encouragement and love those children of the gods, those men and women with charm and brilliance who carry all before them and get all the prizes; but there are some who fail and fall and falter again and again. Some could testify that the greatest power in their lives has been the faith of others in them when there was least reason for it, the faith that believed in them and held on to them when they were in the depths of despair.

Some of us know what all this means in national life. Everybody's spirits go up at a great victory; but how good it is to meet one in the day of defeat, who, not through a temperamental optimism or a facile or ignorant attitude to life, but because of a deep faith in God, believes in God's victory and the worth-whileness of life, even when all its most precious values look as if they are being crushed out of existence.

2. Blessed are they who are not ashamed of Jesus Christ.

We all dislike those who, too blatantly and obtrusively, talk about holy things; but a far more courageous witness is necessary in the places where we work if society is to be leavened by the spirit of Christ.   Too many of us are "waiting" for the kingdom of God.   Too many of us are disciples "secretly, for fear of someone"—maybe the people we live with and work with.   Do the people in our own home know that we are definitely on the side of Jesus Christ, however we may fail him by our moods and tempers at certain times?   Do the people in our office know that we are pledged followers of Jesus? I cannot help but feel that in many an office and workshop the kingdom of God would be tremendously hastened if those, especially those in authority, by some act or word would let it definitely be known that they are Christians.   Many a youngster in his teens leaves school with high ideals and begins his life in the world.   In his heart he wants to live a clean, pure, Christlike life, and that he should do this is the whole burden of the prayers of his mother. Then the doubtful story goes round the office and he giggles because "the others do."   There may be invitations to spend his leisure in places which hold glamorous attraction and much temptation.   To be called a "sport" or "a man of the world," not to be called a "sissy" or a "sop," he weakly starts a course it is hard to stop.   He was a disciple of Jesus secretly, for fear of the "Jews," and the "Jews," or rather the *fears,* won.   It is so very hard to be good alone; and men are taunted, and thought to be "goody-goody," and called the names that hurt so much in youth.   They soon sink to the level of the rest.   But supposing, in that office, someone who really had influence and strength hauled the flag to the top of the mast and nailed it there, and when occasion demanded let it be known that he stood for the highest ideals of life.   Supposing, for instance, on some occasion such a man should say, "That is a foul story.   You ought to be ashamed to tell it, and I won't allow such tales to go round this office," how the heart of a youngster would fly to the colors, and how his mother's prayers would be answered!   Instead of that there is the smirk of semiapproval, the mumbled appreciation, the guilty blush.   The word of protest is not spoken.   It is always a second-rate morality that refuses to identify itself with a noble cause.

3. *Blessed are they who do not try to make the best of both worlds.*

The worst of those people is that the conflict makes them unhappy.   They are not wicked enough to be happy in wickedness.   They are not disciplined enough to find joy in God.   They pass from one world to another without enjoying either.   When they are "enjoying the pleasures of sin for a season," they feel guiltily unhappy. When they watch the carefree sinner, they suspect him of having a better time than they, for all their scruples. They remind one of the curate in Paris who wished he had visited it before his conversion. They are at war within, seeking the best of both worlds. You know the kind I mean. When they are in an environment of worldliness, they claim to be the worldling. They have nothing to do with the church, not they! They laugh at jokes against the church. Then, if they happen to be in the company of churchmen, they say, "Well, of course, you know I have always believed these things myself. I don't go to church, but I am really one with you. I had a brother who once thought of being a parson," or "My grandfather was a well-known Congregationalist," or, "My mother's aunt was a big Methodist." These people who talk like that are chameleons. They take the color of their surroundings for protective purposes. The next night they will dig up a brother who owned a night club, or a cousin who is a "fast young thing" and going on the stage next week. They are not one with us. They are *waiting* for the kingdom of God; and when others have suffered for it, striven for it, and been wounded in serving it, they will claim to belong to it. They will be at pains then to recall even the memory of acts of allegiance. "Lord, did we not prophesy in thy Name and in thy Name cast out devils and do mighty deeds?" And he shall say,

"*Depart*—I never knew you." I would rather have the man who does not stand outside the church waiting for it to rise to that minimum level when it can gain his condescending patronage. I would rather have the man who is as sensitive as he can be to the criticisms that are hurled upon the church, some of them deserved and some of them smoke screens for selfish indifference, but who is *inside* bearing a share of its shame, baring his own breast to the criticisms leveled at it, by his work and influence trying to make it what he can see it should be.

The letters of Winifred Holtby reveal her to have faced the same difficulties as Joseph of Arimathea. She was a most lovable character. Of her literary ability there can be no doubt, nor is there doubt about her goodness of heart and moral principles. One evening she went to a service at which a fellow student of her own at Somerville, an out-and-out Christian, was dedicated, preparatory to going to China as a missionary. Wistfully, Miss Holtby returned to her rooms, and, in a letter describing the service, wrote these words: "The difficulty is to what can one dedicate oneself. I am blown about by a wandering wind of great pity and sorrow and desire, while my weakness and self-indulgence and timidity . . . . keep me tied to earth. . . . . I live in an atmosphere of good intentions about other people's welfare." [6]

[6] Winifred Holtby, *Letters to a Friend,* p. 196.

4. *Blessed are they who offer their prestige to Jesus.*

Don't ever think that Christianity condemns ambition. So long as a man does not climb up by pushing others down, Christianity exhorts a man to be the most useful and influential man he can be and dedicate all to Christ's service. Is that not part of the meaning of the parable of the talents? Mobilize all your resources and abilities, and draft them into front-line service for Christ.

I once heard Prof. Jessop, of Hull, say that there are a great many good people in the world, but so many are not in a position to make their goodness count for a lot. That statement needs modification, but there is much truth in it. Christian young men and women should aspire to positions of responsibility and government in municipal, civic, and national life, so that their Christianity can count. Christianity will spread, not through public preaching and private influence only. It will spread when Christian men and women take office in spheres where words are listened to, where decisions are made that touch even unwilling lives, so that legislation throughout the land provides room for the Christian graces to find expression, and guards the life of our nation from entrenched evil.

We are terribly, frighteningly in the hands of politicians even in this land of freedom. We are ten thousand times better off than nondemocratic countries, but even here we are committed to courses of action by politicians, only a very small proportion of whom are more than nominally Christian. The church's task is not to govern, but to make Christians. But if this is to be a Christian country in anything more than name, then those who see Christ's vision of the world must increasingly take a large and active part in government.

Think of a Parliament where the overwhelming majority of members were out-and-out Christians, no more afraid or ashamed of owning Christ than the Rotarians are of wearing their badge!

I have walked in Joseph's Garden just below the hill Golgotha. I have seen the empty tomb, restored to look as it looked on the resurrection morning. No one can be certain that the site is authentic, though my own mind felt satisfied that it must have been just there, beyond the city gate, below what is now called Gordon's Calvary. I thought of Joseph walking there, and I tried to imagine his thoughts.

He had arranged his life so nicely. He had got on so well in the world. He had become appointed to the Sanhedrin. He was successful and undoubtedly respectable. He was looked up to by all classes. He had made provision for his old age. He had even provided for his burial. And then, in one day, out of a clear sky, all his sheltered, secluded life had been broken up. The shadow of a cross fell over his garden, and that lovely place would now always remind him of the pain of Christ's dying and the mental anguish of his own failure openly to avow his Lord.

He missed the fourfold blessedness: the blessedness of those who at midnight are sure of the dawn; the blessedness of those who are not ashamed of Jesus Christ; the blessedness of those who do not seek to live in two worlds, but are utterly committed; the blessedness of those who lay at his feet all their ambition, their powers, their prestige, and who without being "unco guid" on the one hand, or pining for poisoned food on the other, strive to direct all their life's energies into the channel of God's will.

We shall learn one day that nothing is so integrating to personality as to end conflict by directing all our energies into one channel; that nothing ends worry like committing our whole lives, with all their concerns, to Christ, and making him—as we may, if we heed his signposts—responsible for what happens; and that nothing is so truly our own forever as that which we give to God.

Chapter XII

CLEOPAS OF EMMAUS

GEORGE ELIOT called the story of the way to Emmaus the loveliest story in the world. It is so beautiful and so relevant to our need that I propose we should try to see it clearly. It is related only by Luke, and to read it is like looking at a beautiful picture painted by a master hand. There is an old legend that Luke was an artist in color as well as a physician. He was certainly an artist in words.

How somber is the background of the picture! It is a background of disillusionment and despair. These two who went to Emmaus that dark day had heard stories of an empty tomb, but they did not believe them. Luke says, "These words [about his resurrection] appeared in their sight as idle talk; and they disbelieved them." [1] Luke's medical training caused him frequently to use medical terms, and the word he uses for "idle talk" is *leros* (λῆρος), a medical term applied to the wild talk of a person in de*lirium*.[2] "We hoped," added the two travelers,

[1] Luke 24:11.

[2] Hobart ex Plummer, *International Critical Commentary on St. Luke's Gospel*, p. 550: "Even St. John did not infer from the disappearance of the body that He had risen until he had examined the tomb for himself (John 20:8). Apparently no one had understood Christ's predictions of His rising again. They

171

"that it was he who should redeem Israel." [3]

Can you imagine these two going home, a man called Cleopas and, as I think, his wife? That may only be a fancy, but the companion is unnamed, which might the more easily happen if the person were a woman, particularly the woman who told Luke the story and wanted to remain anonymous. They lived together, which suggests a man and wife. The invitation to supper sounds like a man and his wife to me. Wise men do not invite strangers to a meal without consulting their wives first, especially after an absence from home for some days!

Anyway, watch them going home together in the quiet evening light toward Emmaus, now called El Kubeibeh, the picturesque little village seven miles northwest of Jerusalem in the lovely valley, or wadi, called Beit Chanina. They are sharing their disillusionment, as people do, digging themselves into their despair and justifying it, going round and round, over and over the sad ground again and again, in a morbid circle of mutual commiseration. "Yes, and he said. . . . ." "Yes, and don't you remember his saying this? . . . . and none of it has come true.

---

were interpreted of His return in glory, either with a new body or as an incorporeal being. No Apostle had grasped the fact that He would be killed, buried and raised again to life. They had seen Him dead and women's talk about Angels who said that He was alive did not cancel that."

[3] Luke 24:21.

He said he would rise again, but there was nothing in his promises." Could depression be deeper? He had seemed so utterly trustworthy, and even he had deceived them.

So they "communed together" (ὡμίλουν).[4] It is our word "homily." They meditated and their doubts grew. They questioned together and their disillusionment was complete.

Then a Stranger overtook them. Notice Christ's concern for their mental poise. There is no flashing, blinding light, no sudden apparition meeting them, no unearthly voice. They are not suddenly confronted with evidence that would disable their minds or overwhelm their mental processes. The evidence is such as could be examined. The happening was supernatural, but it was not uncanny. Only afterward did they realize who he was. He seemed just a travel-stained Stranger plodding along the dusty seven-mile tramp to Emmaus. They did not recognize him.

It is hard to understand the body of Jesus after his resurrection. It was like the old body, yet it was unlike it, for Mary thought he was the gardener. The Stranger enters into conversation. He listens for a time, and then he breaks the morbid circle of their misery and mutual self-pitying. "What is all this you are debating on your walk?"[5] They stood

---

[4] Luke 24:14.
[5] Luke 24:17 (Moffatt).

still. "What?" asked Cleopas sadly. "Are you such a lonely stranger in Jerusalem that you haven't heard about Jesus the mighty prophet, crucified by the priests?" Then comes the word that gives us the background of their minds: "We hoped that it was he who should redeem Israel. And here we are three days afterward with nothing but the disturbing wild talk of some of our women who say that he lives. But they haven't seen him!"

What a thrilling story it is! "We hoped that it was he who should redeem Israel." He *had* begun to redeem Israel and *begun with them*. And they were talking to him all the time. We notice how important that fact is for mental health. They were *talking* to him. Jesus never merely "appeared" as a ghost. He always tried to enter into relationships with people. And here he uttered his great words, "O foolish ones, how reluctant you are to believe in all that the prophets have spoken." *All,* not only the glories but the sufferings of the Messiah. "Behoved it not the Christ to suffer these things?" In other words, "Wasn't it fitting?"

You listen here almost breathlessly, for you expect them to burst out with, "No, of course, it wasn't fitting!" Fitting that the loveliest life that ever lived should be murdered by jealous, cruel priests? Supposing you had adored someone, left all and followed him, watched him healing, heard him preaching, seen in him a new glory that transfigured life, believed that he would bring in a new age; and then he had been struck down and brutally murdered by an insane gang of jealous, plotting priests, and someone had come up on the road who seemed to be the only one in Jerusalem who hadn't heard all about it and who had said to you, "But wasn't it quite fitting?" Fitting!

But they do not thus protest. And one of the psychological miracles in the New Testament is that none of the apostles protested. From the very beginning it seems that they never regarded his death as a vile murder. It *was* that, but it carried a divine meaning and significance. God could take even the horror of a brutal murder and make it carry a meaning and a message that were his own. And wasn't it fitting, that when God became man, that Man should know the darkest experience which befalls human nature? Beginning from Moses who had redeemed Israel by that mighty exodus from Egypt, the Stranger showed how Christ also, by the decease or exodus ($\tau\grave{\eta}\nu$ ἔξοδον) he had accomplished at Jerusalem, would redeem the whole world. Luke used the word "exodus" when describing, in the Transfiguration story, what Jesus had discussed with Moses and Elijah on the mountain—namely, the decease or exodus which he must accomplish at Jerusalem.[6]

[6] Luke 9:30: "Behold, there talked with him two men, who were Moses and Elijah; who appeared in glory, and spake of his decease (ἔξοδος) which he was about to accomplish at Jerusalem."

No wonder their hearts burned within them!

They drew near their home on the hillside. With the usual Eastern politeness the Stranger made as though to pass on. They just couldn't let him go. They had been away for days, and the larder wouldn't be very full, but they couldn't let him go. "Abide with us; for it is toward evening, and the day is now far spent." It is dangerous still in Palestine to be out on the roads at night. But far more than that they wanted to hear more. Who wouldn't?

So he went in with them. But a strange thing happened. When the meal was set, the Stranger assumed the rights of the host. He picked up one of the small, flat loaves to be found in every home in the land. Can you sense the tension? Wasn't that a scar on the outstretched hand? When he broke the loaf in half, their minds resisted no longer. We all have little characteristics which our friends would recognize anywhere. He had a characteristic way of breaking the loaf when he said grace. They knew him. "He became known to them," says Luke, "in the breaking of the loaf." [7] Then, having established certainty through their eyes and ears, he "vanished out of their sight."

Back they go to Jerusalem. We need not hesitate to accept that statement. In one of his books, [8] Dr. Hadfield tells us how he witnessed an explosion at a

[7] Luke 24:35.
[8] *The Spirit,* p. 73.

munition factory and "afterwards heard that a woman, after her day's work, had risen from bed, and, in anxiety for the safety of her husband and son, had run practically the whole distance of seven miles [the same distance as that from Emmaus to Jerusalem] to the scene of the explosion in an incredibly short time." In the stress of great emotion, fatigue and danger are forgotten. The sense of excitement breaks through the narrative and possesses us as we read. The lateness of the hour and the danger of the roads had led them to deter the Stranger from going further. That was over an hour ago. Now they race back a seven-mile journey, a rough enough road even in daylight, as I can testify. But the incredible has happened. He *is* alive, unless they are both mad together. Darkness and danger forgotten, they speed through the moonlit night. They make for the old rendezvous. They find the eleven still gathered. It is no illusion. They are *not* both mad. Simon has seen him too. They talked together. Then suddenly, without a door opening, they knew that he was there. In the middle of an excited sentence Cleopas stopped. "As they spake these things, he himself stood in the midst of them and saith unto them, Peace be unto you." The silence was tense. Gradually a Form separated itself from the dusk of the room. "Then were the disciples glad, when they saw the Lord." [9] It was he,

[9] John 20:20.

their dear Lord, back again, incomprehensibly, and in a Form they could not understand, but there and theirs forever.

The story ends in that Upper Room, the first Christian church in the world, with that same Presence seen, unseen, here, there, until for them all he was everywhere. By his appearing and disappearing he had carried them beyond the need of their senses. There was no further need to say, "Touch me not." They did not even need to see his face or hear his voice. His death had made no gulf between himself and them. He crossed it continually and could live in the seen or the unseen worlds at will. Somehow they knew that now he would be seen but seldom. But beyond the need of sight they knew him near— near in the peace that possessed them, and the power that fell upon them, and the joy that thrilled them through and through. The whole earth for them was full of his glory, and his ascension only meant that he went from some men's sight to be available to all men's hearts, every man's Guest and Friend, all the days, even unto the end of the world.

We have spent a long time on the story, but not too long if we have even caught a glimpse of Jesus touching human lives. For unless the Gospels all agree in a gigantic lie—and it is a bigger tax on credulity to believe that than to believe that in essentials they give us the truth, and a truth of supreme importance —unless the finest saints were all deluded, that same

Lord Jesus Christ is still alive and still available today.

His manner is not, for most, that of visible or audible manifestation. His ascension marked, in the main, the end of his ministry of appearances. We are not to rely on the senses. Such appearances would be disintegrating and nerve-racking, hard to weave into the ordinary texture of our daily living. They would further suggest the localization of one who now belongs to all. But for all he is the ever-available Friend. Sometimes he comes in the storm of some great emotional experience. But sometimes he comes very quietly, as he overtook the two on the Emmaus road—so quietly that we hardly know he is there. We are as men who could hardly say when the dawn broke after a dark night of storm; yet they know the night has passed, and they can see more clearly where before all vision was blurred. Sometimes he comes at such a depth of personality that we hardly know that he has been, save that we feel more able to cope with life, braver, quieter, kinder, more loving, more determined to carry on. In the reading of great literature he sometimes overtakes our minds as we read—or as we hear great music, or the spoken word. Sometimes we contemplate beauty, majestic as an Alpine peak or simple as a tiny bird, and find him at our side. Sometimes in an hour of sorrow or loneliness, repentance or grief, when the soul is on a dusty road that seems endless and our hearts are as depressed and disillusioned as that of Cleopas, we find him by our side, treading the same road as ourselves but with infectious faith that lifts scales from our eyes and burdens from our backs and gives us power to run when we were almost too weary to walk. Sometimes the trust in the eyes of a little child seems like the pledge of his belief in us. Sometimes the courage we get from a talk with a friend seems to come through the friend from himself. Sometimes he laughs at us and with us as a lark soars singing up to heaven, and sometimes he sympathizes with us in the soft sobbing of waves upon a lonely shore, as we lift a sorrow to him which we cannot share with any other human heart. In the needs of men he utters his sharp challenge to our complacency, and in the hush and majesty of a starlight night we know his power and serenity stealing back into our hot and hectic hearts. I think he can use any means, almost, if our mood is receptive to him. One way or another, either through new thought, true feeling, or strengthened will, he will come and befriend us if we desire him. And the fact that he has been will be noted, not in terms of the supernatural, but in terms of our own changed attitude to life and to its problems, and, most of all, to the people whom we meet day by day.

We ought, in passing, to realize what an enormous claim this is.

Our spiritualist friends tell us that in certain circumstances, with the help of medium and control, we may make contact with the dead. I do not contest the claim, though some messages are disappointing. But the Christian claim is that *anyone*, without a medium, may daily live in the friendship of that Radiant Person who lived in Galilee so long ago, and through that friendship become changed himself and find life filling with new purpose, new meaning, and new beauty.

Once grant the fact of the Resurrection—we may leave its manner and the problem of the nature of his risen "body" for the moment—and we find no point in history at which we can place our finger and say, "After this no one ever came into communion with him." To do that would be to make the lives of the saints casebooks of mental illness and the highest offer of Christianity for two thousand years a farce. "I offered them Christ," says John Wesley again and again in his journal. Did he offer a dead memory or a living Saviour? The eighteenth century revival certainly points to the second alternative. It was certainly no ordinary ghost story which in the first half of the first century turned eleven nervous men into heroes and martyrs. Later it drove ordinary shrinking people like ourselves to go "shouting a message to audiences as derisive as some men are today, a message punished with stripes and crosses and red-jowled beasts, yet persisting indomitable, on and on down the echoing centuries until a pagan

world was conquered by a handful of Jewish fisher-
men and a great Church raised its pinnacles to
heaven, to enshrine that message flung to the wind
on the first Pentecost—Jesus Christ is alive!" [10]

Many of us feel that if only we could have lived
with Jesus in the flesh for a week we should have
become changed men. A lump of sympathy comes
into our throats when the children sing:

> I wish that his hands had been placed on my head,
> That his arms had been thrown around me,
> And that I might have seen his kind look when he
>   said,
>   "Let the little ones come unto me."

That we cannot do, and the communion that is
offered will vary in intensity, blurred by our sin, our
lack of faith, even our physical and nervous health.
But we have his own promise that if we will make
time, offer the ounce of faith we have, make little
adventures of prayer, not test results only by our
feelings, not decide beforehand how he should mani-
fest himself to us and what he should do for us,
really desire to be made whole, realize that his love
embraces all men—and seek to love them for his
sake—if we are willing for this personal closure with
Christ whatever it may cost us in self-knowledge,
then he *will* walk the pathway of our life with us—

[10] W. Kirkland, *Great Conjecture: Who Is This Jesus!*
p. 136.

even if we have many doubts and many questionings
—as surely as he walked to Emmaus with those two
despairing ones so long ago, and with the same results.   He offers his friendship still.   And to be
received into that friendship is to be saved.   Not to
be at the end of our journey, but at the end of our
wandering.   To walk with him is to find the road
that leads us home.

We could at any rate make a beginning.   For,
miracle of miracles, the risen Christ is waiting to
enter our lives and live them with us.   He waited at
Emmaus to be invited to supper.   To us he says,
"Behold, I stand at the door, and knock: if any man
hear my voice, and open the door, I will come in to
him, and will sup with him, and he with me."

"Any man" means you.   You will not have wasted
your time reading this book if you begin life again
with Jesus.   You cannot make a better contribution
to the new age than to begin there, to bow in sur-
render at his feet, to offer to him the rest of your
days, to follow him in daily obedience.   Christ will
forgive you.   Christ will cleanse you.   Christ will
understand you.   Christ will believe in you.   Christ
will use you.   Christ will empower you.   Christ will
comfort you.   Christ will guide you.

And when it is evening and the day is far spent,
then, at this end of the last, dark valley, Christ will
receive you, and abide with you forever.